The Little Book of Reflective Practice

CH00663579

The Little Book of Reflective Practice is bursting with big ideas which will encourage you to be curious, reflective and courageous in your professional learning journey. It introduces the key reflective theories alongside case studies from educators to show how these can be applied to improve practice.

The journey from being to thriving is set out in several chapters each providing different themes which will encourage you to capture your reflections, record your learning and development and apply theories of reflection to your professional practice. Full of practical guidance, activities and questions to prompt reflective thinking, the chapters cover:

- getting started
- how to write reflectively
- creating spaces to be reflective
- using reflective practice to set targets for your learning and professional development

Spaces for capturing your reflective thoughts and reflective activities are provided throughout, alongside sections where you may wish to stop and engage in deeper thinking. This book will be invaluable reading for early years practitioners, tutors and early years students on level 3 courses and Foundation Degrees.

Annie Pendrey is an Educational Consultant and Researcher for the Early Years and Education sector, UK.

The Little Book of Reflective Practice

A Practical Guide to the Early Years

Annie Pendrey

Routledge
Taylor & Francis Group

LONDON AND NEW YORK

Cover image credit: Getty images

First published 2022
by Routledge
2 Park Square, Milton Park, Abingdon, Oxon OX14 4RN

and by Routledge
605 Third Avenue, New York, NY 10158

Routledge is an imprint of the Taylor & Francis Group, an informa business

© 2022 Annie Pendrey

British Library Cataloguing-in-Publication Data
A catalogue record for this book is available from the British Library

Library of Congress Cataloging-in-Publication Data
A catalog record has been requested for this book

ISBN: 978-1-032-00601-7 (hbk)
ISBN: 978-1-032-00603-1 (pbk)
ISBN: 978-1-003-17485-1 (ebk)

DOI: 10.4324/9781003174851

Typeset in Celeste and Optima
by Apex CoVantage, LLC

Contents

Contents

Acknowledgements

I must admit there are not many acknowledgements in books that I read so it may be that this page is never read either. But if you are here, I firstly want to thank all the people in my academic and professional journey who never quite believed in me or asked me to lower my standards. Without these people I would have not travelled as far as I have, I would not have changed my story on many occasions to be the person I am today.

And to those who have supported and guided me, often quietly in the background, I give you my gratitude and of course a sprinkling of glitter! My sparkles of acknowledgement go firstly to my family, my husband and my children and my mom and dad, all of whom at some point, have guided me through my career. Also, I must sneak in a thank you to my brother for battling and surviving Covid-19, it was in these dark moments I re-evaluated my life and my career.

Further gratitude goes to Lisa Broome whom along with her team keep my professional practice current and full of rainbows.

Finally, there is one more person, that no matter whether I was wiping little one's noses or delivering a lecture has always been there at the end of my bungee jump – thank you Julie Hughes.

Preface: Falling Down a Rabbit Hole

I recall being asked to write my first reflective piece during my Foundation Degree, many years ago now and sat at home just wondering what the lecturer wanted me to write. I recall staring at my paper, as I always make notes first, and almost feeling a sense of pain at having to write in first person about myself, my professional practice, my strengths, my areas of development and in addition having to embed reflective theory.

I still recall the feelings and emotions I felt, to write reflectively felt like I was falling down a rabbit hole, having fallen into it but not quite sure which direction to take to escape and come out the other side with a reflective account. Falling down the rabbit hole is a metaphor for something or an experience that transports someone into either a joyous or troubled state or situation and now as a freelance educational consultant I have reflected myself and considered how I can support others in their reflective journey and so here it is, *The Little Book of Reflective Practice* which sets out to support you in your fall down that rabbit hole.

So, if you are a student on a professional qualification which includes reflection and/or undertaking a work-based learning placement as part of your qualification then this book is for you. Equally, if you are a tutor who is planning and delivering a reflective module then this book will also provide you with some key ideas and case studies to embed within your module content.

Finally, it may be that you merely wish to revisit the art of reflection and reflective theory. This book will enable you to spend time within the themes to both enhance and develop your professional development.

Happy Reflecting.

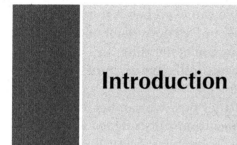

Introduction

Reflection and reflective practice are at the heart of many vocational professions and so I am delighted to introduce you to *The Little Book of Reflective Practice*, a book I envisage you being able to pop into your bag and use for your studies or continuous professional development, using the themes to reflect upon, to scribe your responses and reflections to the vast array of case studies and reflective activities.

This book was inspired by several things, one being my own academic and professional journey having started my career as a Nursery Nurse (NNEB) through to lecturing on a wide variety of programmes both Further and Higher education to Initial Teacher Training. But it was whilst lecturing and delivering reflective practice modules, I became fascinated by not only the structure and content of some of the reflective practice modules but also how at times learners appeared bored by the topic or how it always seemed to be the module that was left until the last minute to complete and submit, often rushed, and viewed as onerous, not quite a reflective journey. As a result, I reflected upon my own reflective experiences and questioned whether at times we spend enough time discovering who we are as

DOI: 10.4324/9781003174851-1

individuals first before we can even begin to reflect upon our professional practice and write reflectively, and that is without the struggle of understanding and applying a few reflective theories in our reflective accounts – all referenced correctly of course!

I began to question further how we can begin to reflect, increase our self- awareness and fully engage with reflective theory, until we are completely aware of who we are as individuals and professionals. Consequently, it could be said that as individuals once we begin this journey of self-awareness and exploration, we then must find or create our safe reflective spaces that cultivate our curiosity, spaces that offer us ease and spaces to be quiet and to think, all of which will hopefully lead to us to being highly reflective in our quest to thrive in our professional careers.

Inside This Book

The journey from being to thriving, is set out in several chapters within *The Little Book of Reflective Practice*, with each chapter having a set of themes, which will encourage you to capture your reflections, record your learning and development and apply theories of reflection to your professional practice.

Your journey of self-discovery begins with Chapter 1, 'Being Me'. Using case studies, creative activities and reflective questioning you will set out to discover who you are as an individual and how this will evolve as you work through this book and your academic journey. You will be invited to reflect upon the types of courage and how you might use courage and other characteristics in your reflective journey before ending the chapter with considering what others may see in you such as your peers, your family, your tutor or your mentor.

Chapter 2 introduces you to the process of reflective writing and the possible barriers to reflection. This theme is where you are encouraged to find your peacock feathers before beginning to consider how we can use our reflective spaces to feel a sense of belonging, ease and peace in order to commence our reflective accounts, journals and modules. You will be introduced to what is reflective writing alongside how to find the time to write following the ripples of reflection.

In Chapter 3 you will begin to focus on the vast array of reflective theories that you can use to support your thinking and your reflective writing. You will have the opportunity to engage with a mind mapping activity that will enhance your note-taking and application of theory to practice.

Chapter 4 then begins to witness your sense of belonging and explores how reflecting with others, your reflective buddy and reflective conversations can all have a positive impact upon your reflective writing. At this point in the book, it maybe you are ready to find your Ikigai, just one of many reflective activities which will help you visualise your future and guide you in your reflective thinking reflecting forward to the next step of your career, studies or employment. Finally, you to consider how you have evolved as a highly reflective practitioner. There is an opportunity for you to capture your progression, identify any professional learning needs and log any continuous professional development you feel is needed to support your transition into employment or future studies.

Throughout your reflective journey, there will be moments when you pause, when you ponder and when you contemplate, these are all moments when you are thinking, when you are reflecting. However, you may come across some other words relating to reflection within your modules and your professional journey, words such as reflectivity and reflexivity.

Reflectivity is where you are submerged in your thinking and use the thinking process to engage and begin to analyse your feelings and actions towards a specific critical incident, whereas reflexivity involves your self-awareness, your awareness of values, beliefs and characteristics and it is only as you begin to reflect in and on action, as you begin to look at your inner self and the community around you, that you can begin to critically reflect about your professional practice. Reflexivity is something we all should strive for as highly reflective practitioners.

How to Use This Little Book of Reflective Practice

The Little Book of Reflective Practice sets out to support you with both your reflective practice and reflective writing as you begin the journey from being to thriving. You will have the opportunity to reflect upon your own professional values and beliefs through to creating your own Ikigai and begin to plan your future developmental needs.

Reflection is very personal and often your tutors will encourage you to keep a reflective journal. However, whilst I have always journaled and used creativity for my reflective thoughts, for other keeping a reflective journal is something they might not be able to find time for or they may simply just struggle with where to start capturing their reflections.

The Little Book of Reflective Practice will support you with a starting point in discovering who you are as a professional and how to begin to write reflectively, whilst embedding one or more reflective theories into your reflective accounts.

Throughout the book you will discover spaces for capturing your reflective thoughts, reflective activities alongside sections where you may wish to stop and engage in some deeper thinking. All these spaces are depicted by icons so that you know this is where you can stop reading for a while and start reflecting upon a certain theme.

Each theme is set out to support you in your reflective thinking and will prompt you to reimagine the situation using your reflective lens and support your journey from being to thriving.

 Reflective Thoughts

Throughout the book, you will find a Rainbow icon in amongst text. This is where you will find questions for you to simply pause and ponder upon, or you may choose to spend more time answering the questions and journal your responses to return to at a later stage.

 Reflective Activity

The thought cloud icon is where you will find questions and/or case studies for you to use to discuss and capture your reflections, all of which will prove useful for written reflective accounts.

 Deeper Thinking

Finally, in parts of the book you will find the brain and cogs icon. When you see this image you will have the opportunity to think a little deeper about the theme and your reflections.

1 Being Me

Introduction

Appreciating and beginning to understand who we are as individuals and professionals is the very start of any reflective and academic journey. The theme of belonging and being me will introduce you to the concept of self-awareness and introduce you to a variety of activities which will hopefully give you a better understanding of yourself and in turn enable you to evolve from being to thriving.

Let Us Start With Bungee Jumping

Have you ever bungee jumped or undertaken an activity which fills you with fear? Whilst, I have never bungee jumped I do believe reflection is a little like this experience, you are fitted out with all the equipment, straps, buckles and a cord which offers you ultimate safety but then you are counted down and expected to take a leap of faith.

This leap of faith is very much like reflection. Reflection is personal and whilst it is hoped it will set you on the path to seek possibilities and opportunities to thrive, a little like bungee jumping it must be **SAFETY FIRST!**

DOI: 10.4324/9781003174851-2

So, as you enter the bungee jump into reflection and the theme of belonging and being me, as best as possible this theme will aim to cater to all your safety needs, alongside the advice not to overthink the process, very much like you would not overthink when your toes are on the edge of a cliff, and you hear the countdown to the jump! But take a leap of faith, take this imaginary bungee jump with me into reflection and believe in yourself.

Theme 1a – Courage

As we take the first tentative steps into reflection and reflective practice, it very much reminds me of my most favourite film, *The Wizard of Oz*. In the film there is a Cowardly Lion who upon his journey along the yellow brick road and into the Emerald City sings to Dorothy, Scarecrow and the Tin Man, 'What have they all got, that I ain't got? Courage'.

But if you have ever watched the film The Great Wizard before the Wizard betstowed courage and a medal upon the lion, the Wizard remarked that the Lion was mistaking courage for wisdom and bravery. Having the bravery to stand up to the Wicked Witch can be alikened to how you have already shown a level of bravery commencing your studies and/or reflective journey.

Starting any new professional or academic journey is scary and so the opening theme for this book is Belonging and Being Me where we begin with exploring what is courage and why do we need courage to reflect upon our professional practice.

So, what is courage? Courage could be best described as one's inner strength to face and control fear, enter difficult situations despite what we may deem to be dangerous, but I also feel that courage is about displaying a level of perseverance, persisting in our attempts to conquer, adjust or reflect upon the situation.

Let us return the lion in *The Wizard of Oz* and it doesn't matter if you have never watched the film, all you need to know is that the lion was scared of his own tail and yet went on to fight to release his friend Dorothy with his companions, Scarecrow and Tin Man from the Wicked Witch. It is here we can begin to explore the different types of courage that Lion portrayed and in turn you may wish to reflect upon your own courage.

It is thought that there are many types of courage which include the following:

1 **Emotional Courage** – this is best described as 'follow your heart', display your emotions and despite possibly not feeling brave follow your heart in the decisions you make. In the case of the lion, despite being petrified of the Wicked Witch, Lion listened to his heart and whilst he felt emotions that were both positive and negative, he knew he had to rescue Dorothy.

 Reflective Thoughts

Stop a while and consider a situation where you feel you may need to display emotional courage. Share with your peers or mentor if you wish or simply have a quiet reflective moment.

Once you have done this, you may find you generate other reflective thoughts as you read more about the different types of courage. If so, pause and capture your reflective thoughts.

2 **Physical Courage** – this is not something which when used causes harm but is the physical courage to persevere, to be self-aware and develop the resilience to pick yourself up and start again.

3 **Social Courage** – this type of courage I believe to be both physical and emotional, the type of courage that

asks you to be you and to display courage in the face of adversity. This is the type of courage I have always tried to instil in my learners, it is the social courage to send an email to organise their own vocational placement, to put their hand up in class and 'have a go' and to ask for help and guidance when needed.

4 **Moral Courage** – we all have a set of morals we carry around with us and have you ever stopped to think how these form part of your moral courage? Moral courage could be described as the type of courage which involves being true to yourself but whilst following your morals, also displaying the moral courage to not only express your own opinions but to embrace the morals and opinions of others.

 Reflective Thoughts

Stop and reflect upon what you consider to be your morals and how these are important to you in your professional journey.

Can you think of a situation where you have displayed moral courage when working with others?

What were the difficulties, and did you have to use any other types of courage in this situation?

---

5 **Intellectual Courage** – if you have read this far in this book, I would suggest you have already displayed courage and now it is time to explore your intellectual courage. This type of courage is thought to be the courage we use when we are broadening our horizons, opening

our minds to new adventures, learning new concepts and later in the book theories of reflection which we can use as part of our intellectual courage as we begin to write our reflective accounts.

Now you have begun this courageous journey, just like the Cowardly Lion on the Yellow Brick Road, there will be many twists and turns and a few dead ends probably, along your path, but this is when you can stop and reflect. Stop and reflect upon how much further will it be and what do you need to take with on your journey to the Emerald City, or in acheiving your qualification.

 Deeper Thinking

How has learning about the different types of courage impacted upon you as a professional?

How might you use these types of courage within your reflective and professional journey?

Have you identified any areas of development from reading this section, if so, what action do you feel you need to take and what support do you need?

Final Reflection

Take some time to reflect and consider the impact this theme may have had upon you and note any questions you may wish to raise with your mentor, your tutor or any thoughts you have as to how you can capture elements of this theme within your reflective accounts.

Theme 1b – Be More Lion

'You will never do anything in this world without courage. It is the greatest quality of the mind next to honour'. Aristotle

Starting any new professional journey or academic study requires you display courage, and even more courage is required along the way in our professional journey especially when things do not go quite according to plan, when we must think on our feet and change what we are doing in our professional practice. So, before we go any further into this theme, take a moment to reflect upon how courageous you have been to already get to this point in your studies.

In this theme, we will explore the many different situations we may face where we need to display courage and how we felt in these situations. For example, how we need to display courage when we receive feedback for our academic work, our observations of our practice and when we set ourselves new targets for development. Much like the opening quote by Aristotle, there is possibly very little that we do in our studies and professional journey that do not need courage, where we demonstrate the ability to undertake something that frightens us a little, something which is potentially out of our comfort zone.

So let us think back to the types of courage, emotional, physical, social, moral and intellectual and having already looked at the types of courage, begin to reflect a little deeper and reflect forward as to how you can be more courageous moving forward with academic studies, vocational experiences, or professional learning. It is hoped that all the experiences on your course or as part of your professional journey are positive, but at times this may not be so and it is here I ask you to reflect upon being more LION, be more courageous and reflect forward.

 Reflective Activity

Stop a moment, consider, and reflect upon a time when you have displayed courage, when faced with a task or an activity that is not quite going to plan.

How did you feel?
Did you want to give up and walk away from the experience?
What made you continue and complete the task?
Can you see where you may have used any types of courage?
Are there any types of courage you feel you need to improve upon and how will you do this? What support might you need?

 Deeper Thinking

Stop and consider some of the next part of your professional journey, your studies, or forthcoming experiences. Take time to consider and reflect upon any areas of your professional practice where you may need to be more courageous, where you could BE MORE LION.

This process is part of reflecting forward and planning how you may need support or what strategies you may need to put into place or which specific type of courage you feel you wish to develop and who you may need in your community of practice to support with this.

You may wish to make notes, speak to your mentor, your lecturer about this or add your thoughts as part of a reflective account.

 Reflective Activity

Read the Case Study, Discuss, Reflect and Answer the Questions. Case Study

*The following case study is all about courage and my own professional practice and aims to support you in discussing and reflecting upon courage and sets out to support you in **BEING MORE LION**.*

I recall my very first observation of my NNEB practice, now known as Early Years educator or teaching assistant, by my college tutor. I had to plan, deliver and reflect upon an activity of my choice and foolishly (now on reflection) I choose to bake cakes with a small group of 3–4-year-olds, what could possibly go wrong!

The observation process I can honestly say I found immobilising, I was so nervous, stressed and at the same time eager to please my college tutor, my placement supervisor, the children and of course myself.

From planning the activity to the actual situation, I felt quite overwhelmed and to this day I recall 'rushing' the activity so much so that the cakes became 'sugarless' in a bid to get the cakes in the oven and the whole observation process over at quickly as possible.

As well as flour, butter and a bit of eggshell all going into the mixture as I was determined for the activity to be child led, one of the children of course wanted the toilet mid flow. Having sent the child in question to the toilet, the child began to scream my name whilst sitting on the toilet, with the screams becoming louder and louder. As you can begin to imagine the little one had had an accident.

I recall the beads of sweat on my forehead, the red rash that appeared on my neck from nerves and anxiousness and having to think on my feet, 'what to do next?' Having finally completed the cooking activity and cakes were baked and the young child in question having been made comfortable once more, my college tutor still watched on and the whole situation felt like days instead of minutes.

I recall presenting the cooked cakes to the children and little noses starting to twitch, whole faces cringe and a couple of body shudders took place as the cakes were licked, nibbled but not eaten as there were truly inedible. (Little note here you will not ever see me on The Great British Bake Off.)

In that moment, it would have been so easy to have felt despair, self-doubt my abilities as a practitioner but instead I internalised the process and with encouragement from my tutor recognised this was a reflective, learning curve.

> *What does my story tell you about the relation-ship between courage and being a professional?*
>
> *How do you feel I displayed courage?*
>
> *What types of courage do you feel I displayed, where and how? Be specific.*
>
> *Do you feel there were any types of courage I needed to develop and why?*
>
> *What other skills do you feel my tutor was able to observe?*
>
> *How could I have used this situation to reflect upon my professional practice?*
>
> *Have you been in a similar situation? How did you use some of the types of courage?*
>
> *What have you reflected upon from reading my personal and professional story?*

In addition to courage, we will explore many other characteristics, qualities or traits that we may need as part of our educative and reflective journey, and you will be encouraged to take some time to reflect upon each of the themes and consider how you can develop these within your communities of practice and in turn become an agent of change.

 Reflective Activity

Courage is not the only quality you feel but also a quality you need on order to be a highly reflective practitioner. So, whilst we have explored courage in depth it is worth taking some time to discover what other qualities you feel you need as part of your

journey towards being a professional in your chosen career. So, the following reflective exercise is for you to stop and reflect upon your qualities, but also for you to revisit this list and activity over the course of your studies, giving you the opportunity to reflect upon how you may have changed or developed.

Start with identifying a list of 10 qualities using the list of adjectives and then you must reduce the 10 you have chosen to only 5.

(There is a list of adjectives at the back to support you with this activity.)

Challenge – list your top 5 and then make notes as to why you feel these are important qualities of a practitioner. You can revisit this list as you begin to work on your reflective accounts. You may also find you display different qualities depending upon the situation.

If you are working with your peers or colleagues during this activity, maybe ask them what qualities they see in you and compare these to the list you have created. Are they the same? Does your peer or colleague see you differently using their reflective lens?

1.
2.
3.
4.
5.

Why did you choose these 5?
Did you have any difficulties choosing your 5 and why?

> *How do you feel these qualities support you in your chosen career path?*
> *Are there any qualities that you feel need developing and how can you do this?*
> *Did your peers see different qualities in you that you never saw yourself?*
> *Do you agree or disagree with these and why?*

Final Reflection

Take some time to reflect and consider the impact this theme may have had upon you and note any questions you may wish to raise with your mentor, your tutor, or any thoughts you have as to how you can capture elements of this theme within your reflective accounts.

Theme 1c – Me in a Box

Having taught reflective theory for several years, I often wondered as a teacher, how you can begin to become highly reflective individuals until you know who we are as a practitioner or as an individual. It has taken me years of self-reflection to realise who I am as an individual and who I am as a professional and I have also come to realise that I can display different elements of me to different people, but one important thing remains and that is to spend time discovering who you are before you begin your reflective journey.

As part of your reflective journey, it is important that you take time to stop and appreciate that as individuals, we are all 'perfectly imperfect'. This phrase stems from the Japanese philosophy of *wabi sabi*, a philosophy which encourages us to take time to reflect and appreciate our community, our world but most importantly, ourselves. Adopting this approach would lead us to think of ourselves as 'work in progress' in both our reflective journey and the road ahead towards finding ourselves as a practitioner who is highly reflective.

It is here that my work in pre-reflection and the many activities I have shared with learners I believe are essential in discovering who we are as practitioners before we can even begin to put pen to paper, or fingers to keyboard and start to write a reflective account.

If you have ever been taught by me, you will know I use a range of creative methods as part of your pre-reflection journey before any reflective theory, accounts or assignments are written and here is one of the many creative ways I have taught pre-reflection, Me in a Box!

Me in a Box is a creative and fun thing to create in your pre-reflection and a process you should revisit throughout your reflective journey, as you evolve, as others see different things within you, as you grow and thrive and how your path may twist and turn and your direction change, so why not stop and create your Me in a Box?

By undertaking this activity, you can begin to reflect upon your perfectly imperfect and consider which aspects of yourself are work in progress.

 Reflective Activity – Me in a Box

What You Need – A Box and Time to Reflect

Take some time to think first who you are as a person and then begin to find 5 items that you feel represent you as a practitioner and think how and why each item represents you.

Capture your thoughts and reflections on a mind map before you add your items to your box if you wish.

For example, one of my items would be lipstick, this is something I always wear when teaching, this item gives me both confidence and a sense of empowerment which are qualities which I feel I need to be an educator. Lipstick was an item that would have been ME IN A BOX when I was an NNEB (teaching assistant) and something which the young children I educated would notice daily and so for me this item will always be part of my perfectly imperfect.

Another example from one of my students was a pair of Mickey Mouse ears, for him these

---

represented listening. However, we went on to discuss and explore the different types of listening we need in our roles as educators and the spaces in which we listen, what do these look like, and what we uncovered was how little time we have in our work to truly listen. This pre-reflection from this activity led this student to conduct research into parents as partners, parents as listening partners. So, take some time to really think and consider your 5 items and be prepared to share your choices with your peers or your tutor.

Me in a Box – Time to Create

My 5 items are:

1.
2.
3.
4.
5.

Why do these items represent you?
Would your ME IN A BOX items be different for different situations, working with different age groups for example – DISCUSS and REFLECT with your peers and your tutor.
Challenge – Ask your peers to name 2 or 3 items they would put in your ME IN A BOX and why? Discuss if you agree with your peers' choices.
Challenge – Ask your tutor, your mentor or coach to suggest an item to put in your ME IN A BOX.

Deeper Thinking

As you progress through your course take time to revisit your box, add items, remove items and make notes as to why these represent you as a practitioner.

Discover who you are.

Discover your Perfectly Imperfect.

Later in the book I talk about the Johari Window, you could use the theory to support your reflections, to look back at your Me in a Box and to think if you have opened up more of yourself to others in your professional practice as your journey continues.

Final Reflection

Take some time to reflect and consider the impact this theme may have had upon you and note any questions you may wish to raise with your mentor, your tutor or any thoughts you have as to how you can capture elements of this theme within your reflective accounts.

Make a list of any further reading or research you wish to do as we head towards beginning to consider starting to write our reflective accounts in the next chapter.

Theme 1d – The Rainbow Educator

The Key Components of the Rainbow Educator

It was during Covid-19 that I became fascinated by not only courage but also colour and during what was essentially a dark and difficult time for many, I discovered the word, 'chromophobia'.

Chromophobia is best defined as the aversion to colour, and I began to consider how I could inject more joy and cheer into my reflective sessions and it is during my time of self reflection I created the Rainbow Educator.

The Rainbow Educator has a set of key components as opposed to just qualities, of which each one is aligned to each individual colour of the rainbow, Red, Orange, Yellow, Green, Blue, Indigo and Violet and each one stands for an attribute, trait or as I like to call them a component of who we are or whom we strive to be as practitioners. So, as we have already spent some time reflecting upon who you are as a practitioner/educator you can now begin to consider and reflect further upon some other components that form part of the Rainbow Educator, these being:

Red for Resilience
Orange for Objectivity
Yellow for Your Inner Strength
Green for Guidance
Blue for Be Compassionate
Indigo for Integrity
Violet for Versatility

The Rainbow Educator is represented by a circle of Rainbow Colours and much like the circle and the arrows, your rainbow of colours is meant to spin and be continuously revaluated. Below is my own created image for the Rainbow Educator.

Having already reflected upon Being More Lion (Theme 1b) and the different types of courage you may need and having begun to discover your professional identity with Me in a Box (Theme 1c), you are now ready build upon all these pre reflections and explore the key components of the Rainbow Educator. The following reflective activities will allow you to reflect upon your strengths and give you opportunities to begin to identify some areas of development as part of your reflective journey.

Red Is for Resilience

Resilience is best defined as having the capacity to adapt in the face of adversity, what we might call the ability to bounce back! There are possibly many occasions in your life you have had to bounce back and there will be many more as you start a new academic and/or vocational journey. Most importantly, as well as displaying resilience, it is important that you take time to reflect upon the situation.

 Reflective Thoughts

The following questions may help you in this reflective journey:

How as a practitioner have you 'bounced back' from a difficulty?

How did you feel?

Think and reflect upon the strategies you used within the situation.

What would you change for next time?

Why was it important to be resilient and who benefited from your resilience?

Do we need to feel part of a community of practice to help us with our resilience, if so, why is this, how does our community of practice support us?

 Deeper Thinking

Consider looking back at the types of courage (Theme 1a) and pause and contemplate, how any of the types of courage may support you in your

> *resilience and approach to certain situations within your professional journey.*
>
> *Spend time with your mentor or tutor discussing and reflecting upon how you might approach your next planned observation or activity and how to demonstrate resilience.*

Orange Is for Objectivity

Objectivity is something we use daily in our practice, the lens we use to view our children, our colleagues, and the world and in relation to Early Years objectivity is key when we observe the young children in our care. We spend most of our working day as practitioners/educators observing young children and it is imperative that we remain objective, that we note exactly what we have observed, we are accurate in our record keeping and use all lines of communication to meet the needs of the young child. Take time to consider moments in your professional practice where you are objective.

 Reflective Thoughts

The following questions may help you in this reflective journey:

Think of a time when you have been objective and reflect upon why this was important for your professional practice.

> *Why is objectivity important in our work with young children?*
> *Reflect upon discussions and conversations you may have with colleagues and parents and consider why objectivity is essential.*

 Deeper Thinking

We all observe others within our working day, our professional and our learning journey.

Stop to reflect upon why objectivity is key when observing others and how objectivity can support future decision making. Share examples.

Consider how legislation plays an integral part of objectivity.

Take time to research or mind map any key legislation you feel forms part of your professional and objective journey as a practitioner and how do you use this to ensure the rights of others are met.

Yellow Is for Your Inner Strength

Any practitioner/educator who works within education needs inner strength to manage your time for your studies, your family and your vocational practice. We need to use our inner strength to help us to find a work/life balance, to help us when we are faced with a mountain of essays or reflective accounts to complete. It is also important to recognise we are not alone, and we have a whole community of practice around us for support.

Reflective Thoughts

The following questions may help you in this reflective journey:

Who is in your community of practice? Maybe draw yourself in the inner circle and your community of practice around you. How does each one of these people in your community of practice guide you and give you inner strength?

Who is your coach, your mentor and how can they help you develop your inner strength?

Think and reflect upon a time when you have displayed your inner strength within a vocational or academic situation, how did you feel, what new knowledge did you gain from this situation and how did this reflection impact upon you?

 Deeper Thinking

Pause, Reflect and Contemplate

Create a list of people within your community of practice that may need your inner strength and reflect upon how you supported their journey.

Consider, is there any training that you require to support your needs in this area and how can you access this?

Green Is for Guidance

If you have just started an academic course, a new job or in an existing role we all need some guidance at some point or other in our professional career, studies or even in our personal lives. As part of the Rainbow Educator, we are concentrating on the guidance we might need in our academic and reflective journey and to appreciate that it is ok to ask for help, support and guidance from you community of practice.

 Reflective Thoughts

The following questions may help you in this reflective journey:

Stop and take time to think of where you are in your academic and reflective journey and note any support you feel you need right now.
Who do you feel you need this support from and how can you access this?
Reflect upon a time when you have been supported or guided and how you felt afterwards.
Reflect upon where in your journey you have guided others, what did you do, what was the result?
How did your guidance support others?
What would you do differently next time?

 Deeper Thinking

As well as the guidance we need as professionals, we may also be in a position within our studies or our vocational practice where we are needed to guide others, where we might signpost or provide support or where we might be a mentor for others.

> *Share an example of how you have given guidance or where you feel this is not an area of your expertise but have signposted others to other professionals or other services.*

Blue Is for Be Compassionate

A key component of the Rainbow Educator is to show compassion for each other, our colleagues, our peers and the young children and families in our care. Compassion is best described as our moral responses to any child or young person in certain situations, for example it may be that as a practitioner you are faced with a situation that requires you to support a young child, adult or family member that is facing inequalities, harm or bereavement. There may also be situations when a child is frustrated by an activity or a toy and loses their temper, it is here our ethical code, our instinctive care turns to compassionate for the young child.

As practitioners/educators, we are exemplars of compassion, but we can reflect much more about how we can demonstrate our care towards others and develop into agents of compassion.

 Reflective Thoughts

The following questions may help you in this reflective journey:

Stop and consider when you have supported a child to settle into a new routine. How did you show care and compassion? What was the impact upon the child? What areas of development do you feel you supported and why? On reflection, would you have done anything differently?

Reflect upon a time when you may have supported a child with SEN. How do you feel you showed compassion? How did you meet the rights of the child? In turn, how do you feel your support helps the child's family?

How would you describe yourself as an agent of care and compassion?

 Deeper Thinking

Reflect upon the areas of your professional practice or the modules you are currently studying, can you link care and compassion to any of the modules?

Can you give any examples of your professional practice and reflect upon how you showed compassion or how you feel you need to address the situation differently next time?

Indigo Is for Integrity

Integrity is the hallmark of any educator. A professional shows integrity by consistently demonstrating their moral and ethical standards and is the foundation upon which your colleagues, young children and their families build interpersonal relationships with you based on trust.

Your course will have its own professional standards, moral and ethical codes for you to follow alongside those set out in policies within your vocational practice or work, but there is one element that is the basis of all this, and this is trust. Trust is something which we need to build with our very young children and their families from day one and is the foundation of our professional integrity.

 Reflective Activity

The following questions may help you in this reflective journey:

How would you describe trust?

Can you give an example of how you have built trust with a child or a parent?

Can you give an example of how you have built trust with your peers and colleagues?

From any of the examples you have identified, what are the benefits for the child or the family when they feel trust within a relationship?

Can you give an example of how you have built trust with your peers and colleagues?

From any of the examples, reflect and consider what are the benefits to you and your colleagues when there is trust. How does trust play a part in your academic or professional journey?

Take time to consider and reflect upon the professional and ethical codes you must follow as a practitioner. Create a list and reflect upon how you display these in your working practice.

Deeper Thinking

How can you show integrity within your reflective accounts? Share an example.

Violent Is for Versatility

The final component of the Rainbow Educator and the one we possibly all relate to the most in our professional lives and especially in education, is versatility. I recall how as a teaching assistant I have supported children from babies through to Key Stage 2 and as a teacher I have taught from Entry Level through to master's and had to be versatile in all my approaches to each sector, to every situation, to every young child and their family.

In most vocational fields, we never quite know what the day ahead entails despite the best laid plans. Have you had one of those days when you have planned an activity, a lesson or an event down to the finest detail but none of it goes according to plan, this is when you need to be versatile?

 Reflective Activity

The following questions may help you in this reflective journey:

Why is versatility an important characteristic for a practitioner?
Can you recall one or more occasions when you have shown versatility?

How did you think on your feet, what did you have to change instantly and why?
Who has benefited from your versatility and why?
Is it difficult at times for you to be versatile? If so, what support do you need to help you develop in this area?

 Deeper Thinking

Having used the Rainbow Educator, stop and reflect upon each element covered, each colour of the rainbow educator and consider your strengths and areas of development in these areas.

How do these key components align to your professional practice and your reflective journey?

How has this theme supported you in considering and reflecting upon your professional practice?

- *Are there are components that you feel you need to develop and how will you do this? What support do you need?*
- *Can you reflect upon one or more of the key components of the Rainbow Educator and include these within one of your reflective accounts?*

The Rainbow Educator is very much part of who I am as a practitioner/educator and having started my career in Early Years I have always kept my practice current and up to date not only from reading, engaging in professional development but also from going into settings and actually 'doing the job'.

This is a very small part of the Rainbow Educator and its key components as each key component then is segmenting into stars and star values and if you follow my work and my writing or even my next book, I am sure you will come to align your practice to one or more of the components or star values. I have been fortunate to enough to train and work with some amazing practitioners/educators who day in and day out place the children at the centre of all their work, and it is here I have introduced many educators/practitioners to the Rainbow Educator, and you will be able to read just some of its impact later in the book.

Final Reflection

Having explored the key components of the Rainbow Educator, this chapter ends with a call for you to consider all that you have explored within the reflective activities, case studies and the components of the Rainbow Educator, so that you begin to increase your self-awareness of who you are as a reflective practitioner so that you can begin to engage more in the analysing and evaluating of all aspects of your professional practice.

This chapter has taken you on an adventure of self-discovery, exploring your values and beliefs, your attributes, your courage and your self-awareness, before you begin to locate yourself within your written reflective accounts.

2 Spreading Your Wings: Reflective Writing

Introduction

Chapter 1 introduced you to pre-reflection and how to take steps to begin to discover who you are as an individual, explore your characteristics, your courage and begin to develop your critical and reflective thinking.

The next part of your journey is where you will begin to transfer your thinking, your reflective thoughts into images or words before possibly beginning your reflective writing and begin to produce critically reflective accounts.

Before you explore how to write reflectively, you will have the opportunity to examine any potential barriers that may hinder your reflective journey, in addition to exploring what a reflective space looks like and how this space can support your thinking and reflections.

The final theme will then introduce you to how to begin to write reflectively before exploring strategies for effective time management and reflective writing.

To be able to start writing reflectively, let us first revisit the word 'chromophobia' and by now you have probably come to appreciate, I love all things bright and colourful and inject as much creativity as I can into my work.

DOI: 10.4324/9781003174851-3

It is here, I wish to invite you to find your inner creativity whilst reflecting upon your professional and learning journey and to be creative in how you capture your reflections. Do not be afraid to display your feathers, which very much like a peacock's varies each time you look at them from a different angle, much like your reflections upon each day of your course or professional learning.

Reflection is very much about using different lens and using these lens to reflect upon our own practice, but I also believe we can be creative and unique in our reflections too, much like the feathers on the tail of the peacock, they are not all one dimensional and one shade of colour, they are red, golden, green and blue and most of all unique, as should your reflective accounts be.

In this chapter and its themes, you will be encouraged to reflect upon how each reflective account you produce will be unique, how you log your reflections will be unique and as you begin to process your thinking, consider how you could doodle, mind map or journal your reflections in the first instance. This is what I believe is the germination stage of reflection, where you can feel energised and let your reflective thoughts flow. The germination of your thoughts and reflections will be followed by assimilation before reaching the stage of completion where what may have started as doodles, or a mind map and then transferred into a final written critical reflection where you not only find but display your inner peacock!

Theme 2a – Barriers to Reflection

'I don't have time to think', 'I don't have time to think about me' are phrases I have often heard in my career from learners and staff, along with, 'I wish I had more time to reflect'. All these phrases alongside my passion for reflection has brought me to the point in my career where I ponder, pause, reflect and contemplate most days the sense of being me, and the meaning of self and how we can use our reflective journey to belong and thrive. So let me introduce you to my brain.

Meet My Brain

If I were asked to conjure up an image of my brain, it is fair to say that most days it looks an entangled mess and if I had to draw it, it would look like the roots of a tree which are entangled and a little chaotic trying find a way to lay a foundation for growth.

But it is when I pause, reflect and contemplate at the end of the day, that I give my brain the opportunity to untangle and reflect, to sort through the day's events, the observations I may have made, the activities I may have undertaken and my writing. It is here I pause and begin to use my journal in order to begin to capture my thoughts, my reflections in and on action and ideas I have germinated throughout the day before revisiting my journal at another point in the week to commence my writing.

Creating a routine and finding time for contemplation and overcoming any potential barriers to reflection will support you in unscrambling your brain, reduce the chaos and open your mind to reflection and reflective writing.

There are several potential barriers to reflection, and it is here I have drawn upon my own personal and teaching experiences to identify a few and in turn suggest possible ways to overcome these.

- **Time** – Reflection takes time and dedicating this time within your daily/weekly routine takes some investment and organisation. It is here you may wish to begin to look at your time management and begin to identify where you have time to process your thinking and reflections before scribing your reflective accounts. (Time management activity can be found in Theme 2f.)
- **Environment** – Finding the right environment for you to study and indeed to reflect is personal and not always easy to create or find but is essential to your thought processes. You may prefer a busy environment whereas I work best in peace and quiet, take time to think about where your reflective space will be and alongside the environment you can then set regular time aside to be reflective. (Creating Reflective Spaces can be found in Theme 2b.)
- **Fear** – As reflection is both personal and there is no right or wrong answers this can create a sense of fear, or lack of disbelief in one's ability to reflect critically. You may also fear you have a lack of knowledge and that not all the reflective theories you come across suit your professional practice. To overcome fear, share any concerns with your tutor and/or mentor as well as beginning to make notes, doodle or draw your reflections as soon as you begin your reflective journey. You will be amazed at the transformation in your thinking, your reflections, your understanding of theory and critically reflective writing by the time your course/module ends.
- **Culture** – The culture we work in can sometimes be an organisational barrier to reflection particularly if there is no time for reflection or there is a lack of support or resources available to you. Building a reflective community

of practice is key in working together reflectively in order for you to move from being to belonging to thriving.

Identifying barriers to reflection and learning has played an integral part in many of my roles in education, and I believe there is so much more that can hinder our full potential in life. As part of teaching and learning journey, I have worked with many learners pastorally and academically and together we have explored many additional barriers to reflection, something I refer to as, 'Where the Quiet Things Live'.

The quiet things are all the extra things that may be happening in our lives, the baggage we may be carrying during our working day and I feel that as educators we need to be mindful of our own and others 'quiet things'. Let me give you an example.

During one of my roles as a manager and initial teacher trainer observing trainee teachers and early years practitioners I began to reflect upon my own professional practice and how often as soon as an observation was completed, I would ask, 'How do you feel?' 'What do you feel went well? What would you improve?' This is something which equally I have experienced when being observed myself as a Nursery Nurse through to lecturer. The sense of rush and urgency for us to reflect and answer questions made me reflect upon how as educators we often give little or no time before, during or after the process for silence and to discover where the quiet things live.

 Reflective Thoughts

So, what are these quiet things?
Where do these quiet things live?
Are the quiet things a barrier to reflection?
Do we all have our own set of quiet things?

In answer to the questions above, I would suggest each and every one of us has a set of quiet things that are present and live in us as individuals every day and they can affect our professional practice and our reflections differently each day.

One of my quiet things are my assortment of 'little bothers'.

My little bothers live in amongst those imaginary roots of the tree in my brain and some days they shout loudly about the list of marking I may have to do, the shopping I need to do after work or they simply say, 'I can't be bothered today'. It is here I wish to highlight to you that my 'little bothers' (just one of my quiet things) are a potential barrier to my reflective practice and my writing and so it is important so that I ponder, pause and reflect in order to reconnect with my learning, my reflections and my work. So, it is here I might need the support of others, or I utilise strategies for time management and writing which appear in later themes in this chapter to support you and myself and my 'little bothers' who live amongst the quiet things.

 Reflective Thoughts

Are there any potential barriers you need to discuss with your mentor, coach or tutor?
Consider booking a tutorial to support your needs.
Use the strategies later in the chapter such as time management and Eisenhower's matrix to support your needs.

Theme 2b – Creating Reflective Spaces

Finding a space to write your reflections may not seem as important as learning how to write reflectively or understanding and embedding theory but I believe finding a space that brings you ease and calm is essential in capturing critical reflections,

We all work very differently, and I know I have taught many students who love to listen to music whilst working, whilst for me this is a distraction as I need peace and quiet.

So, stop and consider what does your space look like and here I do not necessarily mean that perfect home office image we might see on social media but where do you write best and how much time do you have to capture your reflective accounts? Both are of equal importance and as a lecturer I am only too aware that the reflective accounts often become pushed aside for essays and other academic work, but one could argue it is the reflective accounts that truly show the impact of your professional practice. No matter where or what your space looks like try to find a space that creates ease and inspires you to think and write reflectively. How about injecting a little colour, a little more rainbow into your reflective space too, this can be as simple as a selection of highlighter pens – avoid chromophobia!

An array of colours may bring your reflective planning and writing energy, for example, in my weekly reflective journal you will always find colour from pink, orange and yellow to green all of which signify calm, peace and energy.

Moreover, your reflective space and the time you set aside for your reflective writing, stop, ponder and pause to consider having a digital detox during this time, put your phone away out of sight and sent yourself a time limit for writing, ensuring you take regular breaks.

 Reflective Activity

Challenge Yourself

Put your phone down for 25 minutes, have a digital detox and imagine your reflective space or use the time to mind map, draw or note your reflections of the day/week.

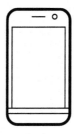

Theme 2c – The Pocketbook Mirror

Having explored and possibly now beginning to address any barriers to reflection and reflective practice and having begun to consider what your reflective space looks and feels like, it is worth stopping a while and further thinking about what reflection is and how it should be part of your everyday practice, something you might carry around with you, something like the pocketbook reflective mirror.

Having started my reflective journey many years ago and to date having taught thousands of students and staff reflection, I started to think about how I would define or explain what reflection is.

Reflection is about looking back upon your experiences, reflecting in the moment but also taking time within the process to reflect forward. Reflection is a process that should allow you to stop a while and begin to process and make sense of the situation or the experience regarding yourself and others. Moreover, reflection helps you to understand the experience and begin to reshape or reimagine the experience, considering your feelings and actions,

Reflection is often aligned to a metaphorical mirror, a mirror that we gaze into and one which we use to reflect upon our professional practice. Most of us wake each morning and look at our reflections in the bathroom mirror and maybe even talk to ourselves about the day ahead, how we are feeling and maybe even comment upon our appearance!

But what of the many other types of mirrors we might use each day, what of the convex and concave mirrors and how does this relate to the pocketbook mirror?

The concave mirror is the mirror that bulges slightly inwards, the mirror a pilot might use to guide an aeroplane which is not dissimilar to how we might use this mirror to guide our judgements and practice. In contrast, the convex mirror, is the mirror which enhances our visibility, the mirror, which is weatherproof, the mirror we might use to both capture the sun shiny, golden moments of our day as well as those loud and thunderstorm days when nothing quite goes to plan and despite the convex mirror, our reflective lens are clouded over. I would argue that you potentially will be used both these mirrors and so should consider imagining you have a concave mirror on one side of your pocketbook mirror and a convex mirror on the other side. This would lead you to imagine this pocketbook mirror being with you all day, sat in your pocket, taken out to capture reflections, all of which should enhance your professional and academic journey before then being reflections transformed into written reflective accounts.

So, Where Do We Keep All Our Daily Reflections?

Now we all have an imaginary pocketbook mirror with its different lens, we now have to consider how we capture and log all the reflections it may capture within our working day, our activities or our observations of professional practice.

Your course may have provided you with specific instructions as to how to log your reflections, but there is always space for creativity and personalisation. Many learners I have worked with start each year with good intentions to start a reflective diary but as their course progresses the journal begins to collect dust in the bottom of a bag and I understand this both as a teacher and as a student myself, so I invite you to be more creative in capturing your daily reflections.

Consider how you might collect your daily reflections so that you can use these in your written critical reflections and more importantly so that we do not forget all the things we have achieved in our academic/ vocational day.

Methods of Reflection

There are many methods and approaches to reflection lending itself to creativity, so do not be afraid to be creative and curious in your approach to reflection. Use the list below to stop and reflect which method would suit you and you can then begin to prepare to capture your reflections.

Journals and Bullet Journals

This method of reflecting offers you a way to record your thinking on the go. They can be journals that are handwritten in a book or in an e-journal. An even more creative way is to bullet journal, log your reflections daily or weekly, you may wish to use a themed approach here, so for example there are some weeks in my bullet journal I choose a theme such as equality and I then might draw a mind map of what I have observed or felt, what resources I need or resources I have seen I wish to adapt or purchase and then I might have a page of clouds to note my feelings. This is your bullet journal, and it is not about perfection or being super creative, it is about having a space that is personalised and you are comfortable capturing your reflections.

Mind Maps, Sketches, Diagrams and/or the Use of ICT

Hand-drawn or computer-generated diagrams may help you with capturing your reflections which you can later return to and review your learning and analyse your reflections. For example, you may wish to produce a Wordle, or you could go one step further and produce a Wakelet or Padlet where you add hyperlinks and share your reflections with peers and/or your mentor.

Final Reflective Accounts

Every course will have its own specifications and academic requirements and it is here you will need to check with your tutor as to what is required for your course, are you producing a reflection or a critical reflection, which needs more in-depth criticality and analysis?

Using your journal, mind maps, diagrams or whatever method you have adopted, you will then need to begin to write your reflective accounts and adding depth and theory, independent research with accurate references and action planning as you progress through your academic and professional journey.

 Reflective Activity

The Pocket Book Mirror

We started this theme with the concept of the metaphorical mirror, but now we need to consider how we transfer the reflections captured through our pocketbook mirrors and what these reflections look like as a piece of reflective writing.

My pocketbook mirror reflections are scribed weekly in a bullet journal of my week. I have journaled for many years and for me it gives me a space to collect my thoughts in several ways, some days I draw, doodle and other days I write a few words or a quote that I can revisit, use in a reflective account or even use with my teaching and learning.

The start of your pocketbook mirror starts right here in this book where you can use the spaces within the book to collect your thoughts, your reflections and is the start of your paper mirror. You can begin to use your pocketbook mirror to germinate ideas before they flourish into reflective accounts which tell others of your reflective journey and how you apply your accounts to reflective theory.

Planning How to Capture Your Reflections

Begin to plan which method you will be using to capture your reflections, a journal, a bullet journal, mind maps or maybe even an audio account.

Make a start and use the following creative thought cloud to process your thinking and to begin to capture your reflections of just this week.

You may wish to come back to this page after reading Chapter 3 and add theory to your reflective thoughts.

Reflections of the Week

Day	Reflections	Links to Reflective Theory
Monday		
Tuesday		
Wednesday		
Thursday		
Friday		

Final Thoughts

At this point you should have taken time to consider and explore any possible barriers to reflection and begun to plan how to log your daily or weekly reflections in a reflective space. Once you have done all of this you are now ready to begin to discover how to begin to write reflectively.

Theme 2d – What Is Reflective Writing?

Whichever course or module you are studying or whatever professional development you are currently involved in, your tutor or mentor will be giving you advice and guidance as to how to capture and write your critically reflective accounts, but this theme offers you a starting point as to how to move from those possible entangled thoughts, doodles and notes to writing your reflective accounts.

Let us start with what reflective writing is **NOT**.

Reflective Writing is not . . .

- A description of events
- An essay which describes something that did or didn't go well
- A list of developmental goals

What reflective writing is, it is emotive, it links learning, thinking and reflections upon your actions. Reflective writing takes time to plan your thoughts following the event and to be clear what is the purpose of the reflection and who is it for, is it for your reflective journal/diary or for your tutor to mark. In addition, consider how your emotions play a part. Reflective writing is emotive so take time to be aware of your emotions before and during writing and how these emotions may become part of your reflection. All these factors help to shape and cultivate your reflective writing as you move the words in your heart, your feelings and actions into words.

As you begin to write reflectively, you may wish to initially mind map your thoughts, feelings and actions, the links to reflective theory, theories or outcomes as part of your academic course before beginning your writing and creation of developmental goals and targets for future practice.

Before you even begin to start to write your reflective accounts, it is a good habit to empty your mind, declutter your brain and so why not try to adopt a new habit of taking 5 minutes to capture your reflections and thoughts – just 5 minutes!

I just need 5 minutes

5 minutes to REFLECT,
5 minutes to CONNECT,
5 sparkly minutes, where I do not quit.
5 golden minutes when my mind does not flit.
5 golden minutes to pick up my pen and recount those
*   reflective moments all over again.*
Pendrey, 2000.

I created this poem many years ago to support a group of learners who were fearful of writing and even more fearful to share their writing and so I created this little poem to support us all. At points in my lesson, I would stop and pause and say it is our 5 minutes to declutter our minds, time to write down your brightest thinking and it was called. 'I just need 5 minutes'.

 Reflective Activity

Just Take 5 Minutes and. . . .

Write down all the thoughts in your head, this is what I like to call your brightest thinking.

Try to use the whole 5 minutes to write all the time without stopping.

In these 5 minutes do not worry about spelling, grammar, punctuation or referencing – remember this is your brightest thinking, use your 5 minutes to declutter your mind.

In these 5 minutes let your thoughts, images, doodles flow.

There is no right or wrong answers, you may look back at the work and connect it with theory or add further detail. You may look back at your work, re read it and never use it again but the motto is 'it is your work and your brightest, reflective thinking'.

As you increase in confidence you may wish to share your writing with your peers. Moreover, it is hoped that this habit of simply taking 5 minutes will set you on the path to more reflective and critically reflective writing. As your writing progresses you may wish to use the list of questions below as prompts for your reflective writing:

What is the issue/topic you are reflecting upon?
Why have you chosen this topic?
What is the issue?
Why is it significant?
How did you feel during the experience? What made you feel like this?
What would you do next?
What information or resources do you need to develop this issue/topic further?
What would you do next?

Deeper Thinking

Giving Your Reflective Writing More Depth

Now challenge yourself and give your reflective mind map and writing more depth using the following questions:

If you were to look at this topic/issue or activity again, what needs to be changed and why?

How would this topic/issue or activity look if you were to revisit it in a few weeks' time?

And now add more feelings, what have you learnt about yourself, your skills, your attributes, have any of these changed? How?

Now consider reflecting forward, how do you feel this reflective experience has helped you develop as a reflective educator/practitioner?

Once you have completed this chapter and its themes, you will be introduced to several reflective theorists and so the following questions will support your reflective writing once you have read and worked through Chapter 3:

Which reflective theory do you feel aligns to your reflection and why?

Is there a particular reflective theory which best suits your professional practice and why?

Theme 2e – The Ripples of Reflection

You are now at the point in your reflective journey where you have collated your thoughts, possibly noted your feelings and your reflections in a journal or within this Little Book of Reflective Practice, you can now begin to think a little deeper about how to approach reflection and reflective writing.

It was this part of the reflective process for me in my own academic journey which felt like a huge 'jump' from gathering my reflective thoughts to embedding reflective theory, it was almost like I was attempting a bungee jump,

Let us ponder, pause and imagine this part of the journey. Imagine you have been offered the opportunity to bungee jump and you have had all the pre-safety talks, you are now wearing all the equipment needed to bungee jump but somehow not quite ready to step onto the edge and take that jump, that jump being the jump into reflective writing and linking to reflective theory.

This is where after many years of teaching reflection I developed my **Ripples of Reflection**, created to help you consider some of the stages you should follow as you approach and begin your reflective writing.

The Ripples of Reflection
Annie Pendrey

The Ripples of Reflection are:

> *Recharge*
> *Reimagine*
> *Reflect*
> *Revisit*

and Keep it *Real!*
So, jump . . . it is quite safe!

Recharge

It is important to take time out after any observation or any activity in your academic journey to recharge your batteries, to clear your head a little and reset your emotions maybe in a quiet space to gather your thoughts before you pick up a pen to note any reflections. Take time to recharge and appreciate all that you have just encountered, appreciate your actions, your emotions and your reflective thoughts.

Recharging and realigning your emotions here is so important, take stock of both the positive and negative emotions you may feel. I would pause, contemplate and make initial notes in the recharge stage ahead of the reimagine ripple.

Reimagine

Once you have recharged, begin to take time to reimagine the situation. This is the time you can begin to consider what went well in your session, what you were unsure of and may need others reflective lens to support you. Reimagine any improvements you might wish to make and prepare to begin to log your reflection. This is where you can also be creative, you could use collage, sketches, mind maps or notes to capture your reimagine reflections.

Reflect

It is at this point within *The Ripples of Reflection,* you can begin to describe your initial reflections of your session or your observation. Once you initially recharged, reimagined and captured your initial reflections, you are ready to analyse and critique much more about the experience and it is here you may wish to embed reflective theory alongside other citations. In Chapter 3, you will find several reflective theories to support the reflection stage of the reflective ripple. Recall how your reflective writing is not merely a description of all that happened in your experience but how you have now reimagined the experience for next time.

Revisit

Revisit is possibly the point within 'The Ripples of Reflection' that may take you more time.

You should now take the time to revisit your reflective account, to proofread your work and to maybe share your work with your peers and/or your coach or mentor. I am sure you have handed in work before and it has been returned to you with spelling errors corrected that you maybe never saw, a little like looking in the kitchen drawer for keys and you just cannot find them but someone else comes along and finds them immediately! The point here is sometimes we just can't see things for looking so start to feel comfortable revisiting your work and asking others to revisit it too.

Ask your observer to spend time with you talking through your reflective account and listen to their account of the session, take notes of their revisiting of the situation, capture their lens – there may be something you have missed and can now revisit and add to your reflection. If so, then you will need to revisit and amend your written reflection and do not forget to proofread once more. This is a point in the reflective ripple where you should use your reflective buddy.

Finally, there is Keep it **REAL!**

Reflective practice is a journey as is your reflective writing and here we could almost create a hashtag #keepitreal. Whilst your tutors will want to read an academic reflection which has theory embedded, they will also want you to be honest and transparent and say it as it is, the reality of the situation, how things really are, how you really felt (do not forget those feelings) and what inevitably went wrong. As an early year's practitioner, I recall planning an experience that my mentor would be observing and play out the situation in my head. The imaginary experience was always outstanding of course when this was so not the case!

In the Keep in Real stage of the reflective ripple, what really happened, was I would have young children who were more interested in looking out the window because the grass was being cut during the observation or children who sneezed the entire contents of their nose across the table or suddenly it was too late for the toilet . . . oops! All of this is reality and very much part of making me the Rainbow Educator I am today.

Theme 2f – I Do Not Have the Time to Think!

As well as creating the reflective space, it is worth taking time to find time so that you can say to yourself I do have the time to think!

This seems an ironic thing to say but most of us I am sure procrastinate and find ourselves finding other things to do when we should be studying, or we simply cannot find the time in our schedules, or we have some of those quiet things we explored earlier in the chapter that are potential barriers. This is where a collection of strategies such as time management study, or a matrix used to identify what is important and urgent for you to complete through to using an approach to support you with your reflective writing will hopefully stop you saying, 'I do not have the time to think!'

Reflective Activity

Time Management

Use the following instructions and template to help you plan your time management. You may need to do a new one each week as we all have very different lives and schedules.

Create a calendar.

Schedule in events that take place weekly such as your lessons or weekly/daily commitments.

Find the Time. Are you an owl or a lark? I am a lark, this is to say that my best thinking is early in the morning, often before everyone else in the house gets up, so for me I would block out early mornings as my best time for my reflective writing.

Prioritise the work you need to complete in chronological order and add mini tasks to your time management schedule.

Revise your schedule weekly as and when you need to plus do not forget work/life balance and time for you and TIME FOR SLEEP.

Days	AM	PM	EVE

Reflective Activity

Eisenhower's Matrix

Now you have found time to set aside for your reflective writing, you could go one step further and using Eisenhower's Matrix you could look at your day, your week and using the matrix decide what is and is not urgent, important and not important helping you to prioritise your work and life using the do, decide, delegate and delete.

	URGENT	NOT URGENT
IMPORTANT	DO	DECIDE
NOT IMPORTANT	DELEGATE	DELETE

Deeper Thinking

Do you need support in any areas of the matrix?
Who can support you in the delegation of jobs,
roles, or tasks? Do you need to book an appoint-
ment with your mentor, coach or tutor to discuss
your matrix?

The Pomodoro Technique

Pomodoro, an Italian word for tomato and the pomodoro technique devised by Francesco Cirillo in the 1980s is a time management method you could use to support your reflective writing.

Having identified the time you have available to work, the space in which you will be working and having possibly organised and prioritised your urgent and non-urgent tasks, here is a technique you may wish to use to support your reflective writing.

Some of you may not be aware of kitchen timers which were shaped like fruit and veg but the red tomato was (and maybe still is) one of them and the principle of the pomodoro technique is that you set the timer for 20 or 25 minutes (you decide) and this is where you work without interruption. After this time, you STOP and take a five-minute break. Of course, today, you may wish to use your mobile phone, but the principal is the same and it is thought that by setting yourself a time and a dedicated task for each time you will train your brain to focus.

Your five-minute break is essential, and you should use it, to stand and move, to reset your thinking and reflective thoughts before bringing your full attention back to the next pomodoro.

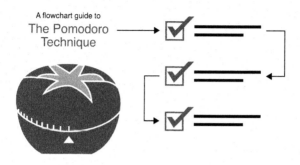

Final Thoughts

We started this chapter with considering the potential barriers you might face as part of your reflective journey and have now explored how to begin to write reflectively in a reflective space whilst possibly using some time management and writing strategies to support us in using the Ripples of Reflection.

Take some time to reflect and contemplate in your reflective space as to how you can use your time to Recharge, Reimagine, Reflect, Revisit and having set the time aside . . . keep it Real as you begin the next phase of your journey where you will ponder and pause and begin to understand and use reflective theory within your reflective accounts.

3 Ponder and Pause a While in the Gallery of Theorists

Introduction

As you enter Chapter 3, use your imagination and imagine you have stepped into an art gallery and like most galleries it has a certain smell, its usually a vast and open space but looking at you from every angle are images and in this case it is a collection of reflective theorists that you will gaze at, read the blur and possibly move onto the next until you connect with a theorist form the gallery that resonates with you. A theory that you gives you a lightbulb moment, a theory that you almost say to yourself that is exactly what happened, that is exactly what I do!

After exploring all the gallery of theorists, this chapter then invites you to be creative in your note-taking and introduces you to the theory tree.

So, welcome and step inside Chapter 3 and the gallery of theorists.

DOI: 10.4324/9781003174851-4

Theme 3a – Brookfield

Having begun our reflective journey with considering who you are as an individual and a professional you are now ready to begin to consider how your reflection of yourself is viewed by others and how we use others lenses to support us in our reflections and our reflective journey. Brookfield (1994) suggests that an outstanding practitioner is a highly reflective one, meaning that we should view our professional practice using others' lenses to inform, support, guide and improve our practice. For example, if you imagine you are being observed and afterwards you receive feedback form your mentor, it is how you use this feedback, their lenses to reflect further upon how the observation went, what you did well and what you might improve next time.

Brookfield's reflective theory suggests that as practitioners we need to reflect using four different lenses and it is all four lenses of Brookfield's theory are thought to give us a different perspective of a situation, an activity or an event that will inform your practice and allow you to reflect forward.

The Four Lenses Are

1. Our Self Lens

Our self lens is our autobiographical lens, in other words the things we see, view and reflect upon in our daily practice is our self lens. So, imagine, observing an activity or a colleague and you must retell the story, the situation, this would be just your perspective – your Self Lens.

2. The Child's Lens

The child's lens is whereas practitioners we try to capture the child's viewpoints, their perspectives of the activity you may have planned for example. You can then use the child's lens to guide you in your reflection and reflective accounts. Consider if the child lens and their reflections match your self lens.

4. Our Colleague's Lens

A colleague's lens is anyone who supports you or is part of your learning and/or professional journey. Your colleagues' lens can be anyone from your peers to senior management, anyone in your community of practice, anyone who is involved in your reflective journey. At some point in your learning and development, it is beneficial to receive feedback from your colleagues to inform your reflections and your reflective journey.

Whilst you are studying your colleagues' lens maybe your coach, your tutor, your assessor and or supervisor who will offer you verbal and written feedback, all of which are invaluable in reflecting forward and creating goals.

5. Literature Lens

Consider how much literature both legislation and theory you will cover or have already covered in your academic studies and professional practice. This is the literature which Brookfield purports will inform your literature lens where you will reflect upon how literature may inform, amend and/or influence your practice.

Reflective Activity

So let us stop and think how we can use all four lenses in our reflective accounts.

Case Study

In one of my roles, I was fortunate to work with the Speech and Language service and supported several children with diverse needs. One child was an elective mute and from Nursery to Year 2 never spoke a single word in the school grounds but as soon as this child left the school gate would vocalise with her parents.

I worked with this child for several years with each school day following a programme set for us by the Speech and Language Therapists. I would attend meetings with parents, the educational psychologists, the speech and language, the teacher, the SENCO and of course the child in question, all of us bringing our different perspectives to the work we were doing with this young child and aligning our work to inclusion policies and what we know today to be the Equality Act 2010.

It was four years of individual sessions Monday to Friday before this child spoke one word to me and I recall it to this day. The word was 'tree' loud and clear as we looked out of the window one windy day during our session together. I recall wanting to scream and shout with joy but remained calm and acknowledged that it was indeed a tree. This was the start of another long journey of trust and work before this child entered Key Stage 2 as a communicator. To this day it remains one of the highlights of my career.

But let's stop and reflect how Brookfield's lens were used in my work.

Questions for Reflection

Can you see where Brookfield's four lenses might be used in this case study?

Which lens do you feel was the most difficult to capture and how would you overcome this? What strategies might you use?

Why was the colleague's lens important when working with this child, what perspectives would each one bring to this case study and how would their perspectives influence your work and your reflections?

Where do you feel the parent's lens is within Brookfield's theory and why must we work with and use the parent's lens?

How does the literature lens feature within this case study?

Give some examples of how the literature would have influenced my work with this child.

 Deeper Thinking

Use this space to stop and identify all the literature, legislation, frameworks and policies you use within your professional practice.

Think and scribe some notes how each one influences your work and your self lens.

Reflective Activity

Planning Your Reflective Accounts

Use the table below to think of an activity, and observation or a time you wish to reflect upon. Before you begin your reflective writing, consider how you can apply Brookfield's lens and use the table below to draft your reflective account.

Planning Your Reflective Account – Using Brookfield's Theory	
Self Lens	*Child's Lens*
Colleague's Lens	*Literature Lens*
List your reading and citations.	
List support you need.	
List any further reading that you need to do.	

As you begin to identify more with Brookfield's reflective theory, it may be that like me you start to explore many more possible lenses within each four lens. This is something I have explored within the self lens and continue to do so in my professional and academic journey. It is here I will introduce you briefly to my inquisitive lens. Whilst it could be argued that the inquisitive lens is just the self lens according to Brookfield, I believe that there are a variety of unique and personalised sub self lenses that we could add to our reflective lenses, the inquisitive lens being just one of them.

Exploring the inquisitive lens alone, it is this additional part of my self lens that has witnessed my involvement in many research projects and opportunities to date, and I also believe it is this very lens that has given me the courage to change direction in my career path over the years. Moreover, my fascination for reflection and exploration of sub self lens leads me to reflect upon how much as educators or practitioner's, we use our inquisitive lens in our daily practice, often without even knowing or taking time to think about it.

Within my Early Years sector, I have reflected upon how daily as practitioners we often work with our teams to create and provide activities and resources that ensure our young children are absorbed in fascination, imagination, curiosity and much more, but how often do we all as educators take time to reflect upon what fascinates us and what is live within us that day, week, or month: our inquisitive lens? It may be that as we begin to explore our sub self lens, we revisit our time management, so we find the time to pause, reflect and explore further sub lenses, give ourselves more time to be curious about our journey and our reflections. Take time to stop and ask ourselves, do we need to explore our inquisitive lens much more so that we can begin to scribe more critical reflections, create action plans and identify our developmental needs, what is it that is currently intriguing you and what do we want to learn more about? Go on be INQUISITIVE!

 Reflective Thoughts

Do you feel Brookfield's self lens has sub lenses?

What would these be? Create a list and then add notes as to how you might display some of these sub self lenses.

Reflecting upon the inquisitive lens, what are you currently inquisitive about in your professional field?

How can you access training to develop in this area?

What support do you feel you need?

How do you feel you use your inquisitive lens in your day-to-day professional practice? Give examples.

Theme 3b – Schon

As practitioners, we often follow the lead of children or our young people in their work changing and adapting our approaches, trying something new and deciding on which approach works best, often 'thinking on our feet'.

Schön (1983) is a theorist that has made a significant contribution towards guiding us in our understanding and application of theory to our professional practice. Schön (1983) suggests that we **reflect-in-action** and this is followed by our **reflection-on-action**.

Let us stop and consider what these terms mean and how they apply to your professional practice and your reflective practice.

Schön

Reflection **IN** action	This is where you will be reflecting as something happens, that in the moment occurrence. It is here that Schön asks you to: <ul><li>Think what is happening, consider the situation.</li><li>Now react and think on your feet, decide how to react and what needs to be done next.</li><li>Then act immediately to the situation.</li></ul>
Reflection **ON** action	This is where you will be reflecting after the situation. It is here that Schön asks you to: <ul><li>Revisit the situation and consider what needs changing.</li><li>Reflect and decide what you would do next time in this situation and act upon it.</li></ul>

The process of reflecting-in-action and reflecting-on-action asks you to notice what is happening 'in action', reflect upon the situation and almost reimagining the situation, the 'on-action' and adopt a new perspective, build new understanding, and apply this to the situation. At the same time, take time to consider your feelings about the experience and what support you might need moving forward in your learning.

Further reflection-on-action is the time you spend looking back upon the situation, and potentially spending 5 minutes to capture your reflective thoughts in your journal, capturing the positives and potentially some areas of development ahead of writing a reflective account.

Reflective Thoughts

Take some time to pause and ponder upon a recent situation where you can apply Schön's reflective theory.

Note your reflection-in-action.

Give specific examples. Share these with your peers or tutor/mentor.

Note your reflection-on-action.

Give specific examples, and share these with your peers or tutor/mentor.

Reflective Activity

Yw before transferring to a written reflective account.

Schön Reflective Activity		Your Brightest Thinking
Reflection IN action	This is where you will be reflecting as something happens, that in the moment occurrence. It is here that Schön asks you to: ● Think what is happening, consider the situation. ● Now react and think on your feet and decide how to react and what needs to be done next. ● Then act immediately to the situation.	
	This is where you will be reflecting after the situation. It is here that Schön asks you to: ● Revisit the situation and consider what needs changing. ● Reflect and decide what you would do next time in this situation and act upon it.	
Areas to Develop.		
Support I need.		
Further Reading or quotes I can use to support my future reflective account.		

Reflective Activity

The following case study is from Tina Reilly who started her career as an NNEB, what we might now know as an Early Years Practitioner. Read her case study and then answer the reflective questions.

Case Study – Story Time

In the early days of NNEB training there was little mention of the term reflective practitioner, nevertheless on closer inspection the impact of my own early experience has had a major impact on my career as a Nursery Nurse but also on my current practice as a teacher of early years educators today.

I recall as a first year and 'fresh out of school' NNEB trainee, the daily routine of 'story time', the initial encounter of this had filled me with dread to say the least and I remember in the beginning how truly challenging I found this part of my role.

As story time approached, I became more nervous, and my face would become bright red as my cheeks became 'rosier' by the second. To make things worse and to add to my fear and angst it was observation day and my lecturer from college had arrived to observe me.

On this occasion, the experienced NNEB enthusiastically announced to the nursery children that I had a lovely story to share with them and gestured to me to continue the story time. The children stared in anticipation of an exciting story time ahead, however like a rabbit in the headlights, I froze in fear at the thought of this never-before-experienced task.

I picked up a story that looked mildly familiar from the shelf and began to read with a quiet quivering voice. The children fidgeted, fussiness and silliness increased rapidly and developed into what can only be described as a chaotic mayhem and the story time was becoming a shambles.

It was 'fight or flight', I had to think on my feet to save this situation, I stood up and to everyone's amazement (including mine) bravely and very loudly began to sing, 'if you're happy and you know clap your hands', clapping my hands enthusiastically in a vain attempt to re-engage the nursery children who by now were giggling, jumping and rolling around play fighting in the book corner. The sight and sound of the energetic and slightly frantic NNEB began to draw the children to join in one by one with the actions and singing to re-engage them once more.

After this experience, I considered how I could approach story times to develop my skills and confidence to improve the children's experience.

My own early experiences have had a tremendous impact on my teaching today, I consistently empathise with learner's emotions and personal challenges and provide support, knowledge and practice to guide them to develop and assert their skills and competence in a holistic and purposeful way to enable individual growth.

Reflective Questions

Where do you feel Tina applied Schön's reflective theory?
Where did Tina think on her feet and what was the outcome?
Where did Tina reflect in action?
Where do Tina reflect-on-action?
What was the outcome of this thinking and reflecting?
Was Tina able to identify her future needs and what do believe these were?
By reflecting in and on action, what were the outcomes for the children?

Tina Reilly is an Early Years Lecturer and External Assessor (FSET ATS CTeach)

 Deeper Thinking

Look back at Theme 1a, what types of courage do you feel Tina displayed within this situation?
Research empathy and/or emotional intelligence – how do these topics potentially impact upon Tina's professional practice today from having had this experience of reading to young children?

Schön (1983) also asks us as reflective practitioners to consider that our practice can be muddy and at times, we can become a little stuck. This is what Schön (1983) would refer to as swampy lowlands. When I imagine swampy lowlands and reflection, I consider Schön's reflection-in-action as almost giving ourselves permission to get things wrong, to become stuck and if we relate this to the swampy lowlands we might be 'stuck' for a while, we might not be able to climb out of the muddy mess alone, but we need others to support us in our reflections, our professional practice and our reflection-on-action.

I imagine Schön gave us this image to support us in our 'have a go approach', to support our having, 'to think on our feet' so that one day we might not need a pair of wellington boots as our muddy swamp becomes a lot clearer.

Theme 3c – Gibbs

As part of our gallery of theorists is Graham Gibbs and here you can begin to consider being creative by maybe drawing his reflective cycle and making notes for each of the 6 stages of the reflective cycle. Gibbs (1998) reflective cycle is believed to encourage you to think more systematically about the elements or phases of an experience or activity you have undertaken as you pass through the 6 stages and many learners find it useful to answer the questions on the cycle as they build their reflective account and begin to become familiar with this theoretical model.

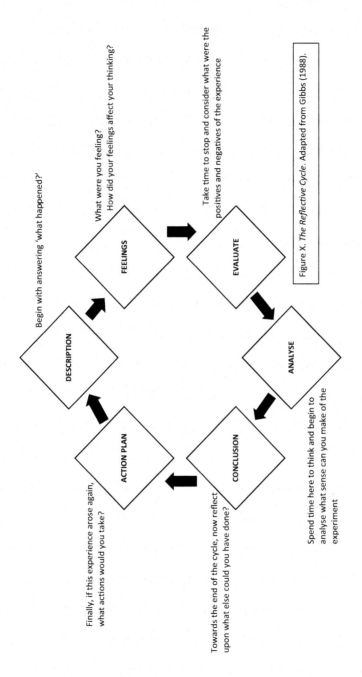

Figure X. *The Reflective Cycle.* Adapted from Gibbs (1988).

Gibb's Reflective Cycle

Stage 1 Description – What Happened?

Before you begin stage 1, I think it is useful to pause and gather your thoughts, look back at any notes from your journal or reflective notes, gather any notes or feedback from colleagues, peers or your mentor. You are now ready to answer the question, what happened?

Be aware as you begin to answer this question, you should be doing more than providing an explanation of events, you are being asked to describe what happened within the activity/observation and so need to add depth. For instance what learning took place, what areas of development were covered are just a couple of examples of describing what happened in the observation/activity you may have undertaken. You can also begin to think about adding more detail such as what happened at the time during and after the activity/observation, so here you are sectioning the descriptions and giving your reflective account much more depth.

 Reflective Thoughts

Here are a few more questions you may wish to ask yourself.

What happened?
When and where did it happen?
What did you do during the experience?
Was there anyone else involved in the experience and what do they do?
What was the outcome of the situation?

Stage 2 – Feelings – What Were You Thinking and Feeling?

This stage will ask you to reflect upon your feelings and here it is important for you to be honest, for example if the situation was challenging then say so. It is human nature for us all as professionals to display or feel a range of emotions when we are being observed or if you plan an activity and it maybe does not go to plan. You may feel despondent but then you can also begin to think how you adapted to the situation, equally you may look back on your thoughts and feelings and identify how you need to will address this next time you find yourself in this situation. Moreover, please recall and reflect upon all the positive thoughts and feelings you experience, as humans we often do not celebrate our positives enough.

 Reflective Thoughts

Here are a few more questions you may wish to ask yourself:

What were you feeling during the situation?
What were your thoughts at the beginning, middle and end of the activity?
Did you have to think on your feet and how did you feel?
What were you feeling before and after the situation?
What do you think about the situation now?

Stage 3 – Evaluation – What Was Positive and/or Negative about the Situation?

The third stage of this cycle is evaluating, and it is often here from my experience of teaching Gibbs reflective cycle that learners forget to stop and examine the experience. When you evaluate your need to find a balance and do not concentrate on just the negatives as you revisit and reflect upon the situation, but take account of the positives too, this will provide a real examination of the situation before you begin to evaluate it thoroughly.

Examine and then evaluate, if you like, begin to 'pull apart' all the things that went well as we can still build upon these as much as the negatives.

 Reflective Thoughts

Here are a few more questions you may wish to ask yourself:

What were the positives and negatives and why were they either positive and/or negative?
Were there any techniques/strategies you may have used that were positive and/or negative?
What could you adapt in the future to improve the situation and why?
What could you adapt in the future to improve your own learning and development?

Stage 4 – Analysis – What Sense Can You Make Out of the Situation?

This may seem a difficult question to ask yourself and one you may be unsure of. It is in stage 4 that you need to again pause and reflect upon the experience, the situation, the professional practice in which you have been involved. Sometimes, the situations we find ourselves in do not make sense and that is part of our learning and development, but it is important you do step back, reflect and try to think analytically as Gibbs asks you to analyse what sense you CAN make out of the situation?

To help you further, you need to focus on more specific details about what went well and the positives and the negatives and then begin to make sense of it. It is in this section, you should add citations, academic literature and your further reading to add depth as this is an analysis.

 Reflective Thoughts

Here are a few more questions you may wish to ask yourself:

What sense can I make of the situation I was part of?
How can I add depth to my analysis?
What other knowledge can I embed in my analysis?
What academic sources/quotes can you use to support your reflection?

Stage 5 – Conclusion – What Else Could You Have Done?

Stage 5 is where you can now begin to summarise all your learning from the situation/experience. You can also now begin to create action points that will naturally occur having followed all the previous stages.

 Reflective Thoughts

Here are a few more questions you may wish to ask yourself:

What did you learn from the experience?
What else could you have done within the situation?

> *Could you have improved resources, your communication or your planning are just a few examples you may be reflecting upon?*
> *Give details as to what you would improve and why.*
> *What skills do you need to develop further?*

Stage 6 – Action Plan – If You Revisited this Experience, What Would You Do?

This is the final stage of Gibbs reflective cycle and one which is not simply about thinking and reflecting what you may do differently next time you were revisit this experience but HOW you would ensure the action point, the plan you create would happen. This whole reflective process and the 6 stages of Gibbs reflective cycle will begin to see you move from reflecting to critically reflecting upon your practice.

 Reflective Thoughts

Here are a few more questions you may wish to ask yourself:

What will you do in the future and how will you do things differently?
What improvements would you make and why?
What would be the impact of these improvements upon yourself and your professional practice?

Theme 3d – Kolb

Compared to Gibb's reflective cycle, Kolb's cycle has only 4 stages and is often referred to as 'experiential learning', a model which is based on your own experience, a process where you review analyse and evaluate as part of the reflective cycle and the reflective process.

The Four Stages Are Best Explained As

<u>Concrete Experience</u>. This can be defined as LEARNING by EXPERIENCING

<u>Reflective Observation.</u> Defined as LEARNING by REFLECTING

<u>Abstract Conceptualisation.</u> Defined as LEARNING by THINKING before the final stage of the cycle active experimentation

<u>Active Experimentation.</u> Best defined as LEARNING by DOING

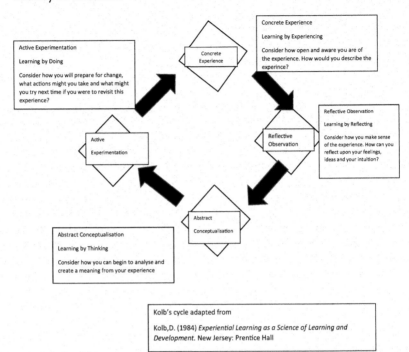

Kolb's cycle adapted from

Kolb,D. (1984) *Experiential Learning as a Science of Learning and Development.* New Jersey: Prentice Hall

From my own experiences, learners have at times found Kolb's reflective cycle a little difficult to apply due to the terminology and so with this is mind here is a summary of each of the four stages to support your understanding and application of Kolb's reflective theory. As you read each stage, you can begin to reflect and make notes about one of your most recent experiences which you could then later capture as a reflective account.

1. Concrete Experience

This is best simplified as 'in the moment'. This is when you are absorbed both physically and consciously in an experience, an activity or a situation. This is when you were either asked to plan or be part of an experience or alternatively, you have chosen to put yourself in this experience to either enhance your learning or learn something new.

If we think back to Tina's case study (Theme 3b) and her story telling, it is here we can consider that she may have initially planned to read a story, to be absorbed within this experience or this may even have been an activity/experience requested by her vocational mentor and/or college tutor as part of an assessment. Either way it is whilst in the concrete experience according to Kolb that Tina, after the experience, would be able to make notes and begin to plot, draft and maybe at first describe how she felt, what she observed herself during the story telling and finally what she thought of the overall experience.

Regarding your use of the concrete experience, you too can at first describe the experience but depending on how much depth is required for your reflective accounts for your course or training, you can always revisit this stage for further analysis and critiquing at a later stage.

2. Reflective Observation

It is now at this point in Kolb's reflective cycle you can reflect at a much deeper level looking back at your description of the experience and begin to ask yourself some further questions such as:

What worked well?
What did not go so well and needs revisiting?
What were the outcomes of the situation? What arose?
What did others see? Were you able to capture other
  reactions?

3. Abstract Conceptualisation

The third stage of Kolb's reflective cycle active conceptualisation is where you will begin to think much deeper about your thinking and reflections that took place in the reflective observation stage. It is in this stage that you might adopt a more systematic approach to analysing some of your previous answers and reflections, but it is vitally important that you recognise the importance of thinking and analysing at this stage.

You can begin to ask questions such as:

> What other methods, ways or strategies would I use if I were to revisit this experience? And in answering this question, the depth is in the why and the how.
> Why do you need to change this and how will you make these changes?

Once you have answered these and maybe more questions you have generated form the experience, you can then begin to consider how you will provide supporting evidence to support your reflections. Supporting evidence such as feedback from colleagues, your mentor or the use of literature and citations, all of which will give your reflective accounts the depth and the analysis that is required at this stage of Kolb's reflective cycle.

Active Experimentation

At this final stage, you will now be able to apply and practise your new knowledge. It could almost be described as learning from your mistakes or taking the data you have acquired from the other stages to move forward with your new knowledge and understanding to the concrete experience once more.

It is in this part of your reflective account you can discuss and reflect upon your new acquired knowledge. This may be a new and improved strategy or approach or a particular theory that has influenced your practice moving forward. It is important to note that this stage is about practising, testing, and trying out the new strategies, some of which will be successful whilst others may not be before you then commence the reflective cycle once more starting with another concrete experience.

Challenge

The challenge of Kolb's reflective cycle is that reflection and optimal learning requires you to take time engaging in all four steps. Do not rush or skip the reflection, observation and abstract conceptualisation stages, where your deeper thinking and analysing takes place. With time and energy dedicated to these two stages, you will find yourself oscillating between concrete experience and experimentation. Oscillating is best defined as going round and round or moving back and forth, where you should be spending time bouncing or testing and trying approaches/strategies until something improves within the experience.

Moreover, it is also worth reminding yourself of how chaotic reflection can be and it is a case of trial and error when testing different approaches to an experience. Reflection can also prove to be emotional, especially when reflecting on an experience that did not go according to plan but hold on, recall that bungee jump at the beginning of the book and recall that reflection needs you to take risks and once equipped with all the correct safety measures and equipment you will become a highly reflective professional.

Theme 3e – Boud, Keogh and Walker

At this point in the gallery of theorists, it is possibly fair to say that you have come to understand and appreciate the importance of being a reflective practitioner, a practitioner who continually reflects upon their professional practice and learning in order to develop and improve themselves as individuals and as professionals.

Another reflective learning model you may wish to use within your reflective accounts and to support your deeper understanding and application of reflection is the work of Boud, Keogh and Walker (1985), which focuses on learning by reflecting upon your practice.

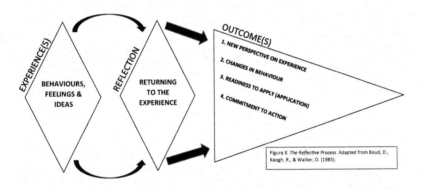

Figure X. *The Reflective Process.* Adapted from Boud, D., Keogh, R., & Walker, D. (1985).

There are several processes to the Boud, Keogh and Walker Reflective Model and these are simplified as:

1. Return to the Experience

Once you have engaged and been absorbed within an experience, according to Boud, Keogh and Walker (1985) it is important that you return to the experience so that you can review the experience, best simplified as replaying the experience, playing it back in your mind and making notes. It is here I feel you should return and replay both the positive and the negative aspects of the experience as we learn from both and can reflect forward and apply new knowledge from both things that go well and things that go terribly wrong.

2. Attending to Emotions or Feelings

Connecting with both your positive and negative feelings within the experience is also part of this reflective process. It is essential that you recognise your feelings and begin to use the positive feelings about the experience for reflection and try to remove the negative feelings that may be obstructing your reflection. Paying attention to your feelings as part of this process will guide you in revaluating the experience, process the events that took place and enhance your reflection, learning and development. Let me give you an example here, as you know I have been observed many times as part of my professional journey and inevitably something always goes wrong. For example, I have had a child have a 'little accident' shall we say, during an observation to one being violently sick and pro-jectile vomiting into my lap whilst I was singing my heart out to the 'The Wheels on the Bus' alongside the story sack I had handcrafted especially for my observation. I can hon-estly tell you I really felt like the wheels on the bus had fallen off during that observation and I just wanted to cry, after obviously washing the vomit off myself and caring for the child in question.

However, instead of allowing those negative feelings to consume me and my reflections, I concentrated on how

I was able to 'bounce back', be versatile and empathetic and move forward in that situation. I don't think any new strategy could be adopted moving forward here but I was able to reflect upon my inner qualities and find the positives, see the funny side I guess of the situation and potentially learn never to wear your best clothes when teaching Early Years.

3. Re-Evaluating the Experience

Re-evaluating the experience takes just as much time as the other two processes and it could be said cannot take place if you do not give enough time and attention to the other two stages. In this stage you need to re-examine the experience from the learner/young child or adult's perspective.

You need to consider the following:

Association – Relate new information with what is already in place, with what already exists. This is further explained as to how you can connect ideas and feelings from the original experience to those that occurred during your reflection. In this phase you begin to see how new information and/or ideas are related. This is a journey of discovery and reflection where you might find your existing attitudes will/have changed as you travel through this stage and begin to make space in your mind and reflections to accommodate new ideas.

Integration

Once you have made these associations, it is here that you can begin to integrate any new knowledge into your professional learning and development.

Validation

It is at this point you can begin to validate which simply means you can begin to plot, plan how you will put your plan into action, how you have reflected upon the experience, associated and integrated your learning in order to now apply this information and/or knowledge.

Finally, it may also be worthwhile examining **appropriation**. According to Boud, Keogh and Walker (1985), any new information you may have integrated now needs to be appropriated. This is best explained as information that is almost personalised and made your own so that it becomes an integral part of who you are as a professional and your reflective journey.

Finally, as most other reflective theories you will arrive at the point where there are outcomes and action to be taken, sometimes very small changes and adaptations or a new way of thinking or an approach that has all derived from this reflective process.

Theme 3f – Johari Window

The gallery of theorists we have covered so far have asked you to reflect upon yourself and not all the theorists require you to explore how feedback can play an integral role in your reflection, but feedback is an important element of our learning and professional development. In turn, as professionals when we receive and react to feedback it supports and helps us develop a greater self-awareness of our professional practice.

The Johari Window was developed by Joseph Luft and Harry Ingham (1955) and much like a window in your home, it has four panes and is a tool you can use to explore your self-awareness and personal development.

Before you begin to explore the Johari Window, it is worth noting that the panes of the window can change in size depending upon the on how well you know yourself and how well others know you, so this may be an activity you wish to revisit several times and in different situations. In addition, the Johari Window is something which can be used to explore group dynamics and team development not only for self-reflection.

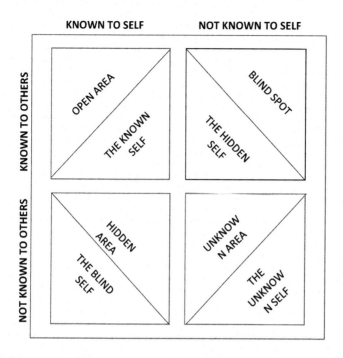

The four panes of glass within the Johari Window consist of:

Open Space or Open Area – Known to Self and Others

This space is best explained as an area which is open and so the individual has knowledge and awareness about who they are, and this knowledge is also known by others. An example of this would be if you have recently been enrolled on an academic course, you and your tutor will be aware of your previous qualifications; this is information known to self and by others.

Blind Space or 'Blind Spot' – This Is What Is Not Known by Self But Known to Others

This space is where information or knowledge about you may be visible to others, but you cannot see it. For example, you may have a mentor or supervisor comment on an aspect of your professional practice that you cannot see yourself such as low confidence when approaching a certain situation.

The aim of this space is for it to be reduced by seeking feedback from others in your community of practice, which will lead to the open area increasing and in turn increasing your self-awareness.

Hidden Space – This Is Known to Self but Not Known by Others

The hidden space can also be known as the hidden self or the area we hide, the hidden area. This is the space where certain things we know about ourselves we keep hidden and therefore others do not know, it is the unknown. This can be things such as certain information, feelings or agendas are not revealed and possibly best explained as when you may have difficulties with an essay, but you do not feel you can let others such as your tutor know so keep it in the hidden space. However, if you were to share or disclose this difficulty you would be opening the open space where this difficulty is known to you and to others such as your tutor, who can then support you further. It is worth acknowledging here how all of us as humans will need a certain element of trust with individuals and team members before we possibly share our hidden space.

Unknown Space – This Is Unknown to Self and Others

This space can include feelings, information, abilities and much more that is unknown to the person (the self) and unknown to others too. This space is possibly best described as the journey of self-discovery and something which your course, your workplace or your training may uncover. A personal example is my creativity.

Creativity is not just drawing or painting for example, and as Art was never an option for me at school it was a skill that was unknown to me and unknown to others as I was never able to display this in my school years. However, during my Early Years vocational training I was set the task of creating many activities for young children and it is fair to say that it was both my college and school placement that nurtured my creativity which proved to be a skill that had been unknown to me and others such as my tutors and mentors. However, can I add once this was known, I was the Nursery Nurse who was always called upon to draw, paint and most definately sprinkle glitter over a few creative projects.

Using the Johari Window

When using the Johari Window, it is your personal choice as to the amount of self- disclosure you choose to engage with, and this is an activity aimed at your professional growth and development. Equally, any feedback you receive from others during the exercise should be open, honest and helpful in guiding your growth and reflection. It is also worthwhile reminding us that the Johari Window is an approach that should guide you in reflection and the development of your self-awareness and any feedback should leave you feeling insightful and reflective about who you as an individual and your professional practice. There are many ways to use the Johari Window and your tutor/mentor or team may use it with you individually or in a group/team setting, but for some self-reflection you could try the following Reflective Activity.

 Reflective Activity

Using the Johari Window

Before you start and the first time you undertake this activity, choose one or a few peers you trust and be ready and open for other perspectives and feedback.

Using the list of adjectives at the back of the book, take time to read them and highlight between 5–10 that you think best describe you.

Now ask your peers to do the same. They now must use 5–10 adjectives they feel best describes you.

Share the words both you and your peers have identified. Place words that both you and your peers have selected in the OPEN space.

Place words that only you selected in the HIDDEN space.

Place words that your peers selected but you did not in the BLIND space.

Any words left you can place in the UNKNOWN space.

Review and reflect upon the words in all the spaces and maybe ask yourself the following questions: How does your view of you align with your peers? What do they see that you do or do not? How open do you feel you are? Are there any surprises? What are these and how do you feel?

Finally, maybe you wish to spend some further time to reflect and review this activity. You may want to journal any reflections, feedback or adjectives you need to develop, discuss further with your peers or mentor/tutor or reflect upon further.

Theme 3g – Theory Trees

We started this chapter using our imagination and imagining we were inside a gallery and that you would be walking through the gallery looking and reflecting upon each theorist on display. As you exit the gallery it is now time to reflect upon how you might use each theorist within your reflective accounts.

There are several theoretical reflective theories that could be applied to your professional practice, to be used as part of your thinking during your working day but moreover each theorist can be used for you to begin to plan, draft and write your reflective accounts. It is here that as a lecturer I would often find learners become fearful as to which theorist to use or begin to explain the theory as opposed to use the theory to align to and support their thinking. In order to support you in choosing and applying a theorist to your reflective accounts I have created theory trees which might spark your creativity, self reflection and support you in cementing theory to practice.

Much like a tree has roots so does all the work we do each day in our sector, and so as part of my teaching I devised a creative way for my learners to both identify, explain, analyse and most importantly apply theory to their professional practice and so here is the theory tree.

The theory tree is used for each theory that may be taught in your sessions or from the notes you take from this book or further research. The objective is for you to use the tree continuously as part of your mind mapping, note-taking and further research. Each tree could be used as part of your reflective diary or journal or be even more creative and devise your own.

Reflective Activity

How to Use the Theory Tree

On the trunk of the tree scribe the name of the reflective theory you wish to explore i.e. Brookfield.

Then on each branch scribe what you understand about this theory. Each branch should have a different aspect of the reflective theory, so for example, you may label each branch with Brookfield's Lens.

Each leaf is then an example from professional practice, a reflection from the day or an activity or observation, for example you may have had. Your examples would be what you feel you could reflect upon in your reflective account.

The roots of the tree can be used in several ways, maybe to note any fears, or support you need reflecting forward. You might wish to use the roots to scribe positives from your reflection or create a set of action points. One group of my learners decided that the roots would be for adding journals, reading lists and references as roots connecting their learning. This is where you can not only be creative but reflective.

Example – Brookfield Theory Tree

Theme 3h – Theory and Practice

Introduction

You have now reached the part of the journey where you have explored lots of pre-reflection activities, discovered which way suits you best to capture your reflections and how to start writing your accounts.

Chapter 3 has also introduced you to several reflective theories and so now it is important that you can begin to embed theory into your professional practice and show how you do this within your written accounts. This is potentially one of the hardest parts of your academic journey and so I have developed a table which I hope will support you as you begin to collate all your reflections, review your knowledge, identify and relate to certain reflective theorists as you begin to draft and then write your critically reflective accounts.

Planning Your Draft Reflection

Reflecting upon your professional and vocational practice supports you in approaching and preparing your critical reflections and it is hoped that it is here in your journey that you can begin to see and feel the value of your training and academic studies.

The next step and potentially the most difficult is embedding the theory you have learnt to the vocational practice, and this is where the value of your reflective journal, notes or sketches will be of great value.

Reflective Thoughts

Take some time before you start your draft to look back at your journal and begin to ask yourself some of the following questions:

What am I choosing to reflect upon? What is the issue or the topic? How does this align to my studies? What criteria am I covering?

What evidence do I have to include in my reflection?

Can I support my reflective account with quotes from any observations or comments from my mentor?

How can I relate my reflection to one or more reflective theories?

Do I need to read more about a reflective theory or the issue before I begin to write my reflective account?

Do I have enough evidence for this reflection? Will I have areas I can identify that I still need to reflect forward upon?

Will this reflection give me some areas to develop, goals I can set?

What did I struggle with the last time I undertook this activity and how have I improved?

How have I incorporated what I learned? If not, what additional support do I need? How will I gain this support, what do I need to do so that I reflect forward?

Have I thought about my feelings within this account?

What will I do next time? How will I do this?

This seems an awful of questions, but it is worth taking time to answer some or all of these before you begin to draft your reflective account as the account should inform your future practice. The table below will help you gather information, self-assess, review, reflect and set goals.

Remember a reflective account is not a descriptive of events or a list of goals and your tutor will support you further to ensure you meet your specifications, but you also can look back at Chapter 2.

Final Thoughts

At this stage in your journey, you should now be ready to draft and write your reflective accounts, embedding theory to practice and practice to theory. It maybe you have really identified with one reflective theory and so should now consider conducting some further research on not just one but all the reflective theorists and be able to discuss, review and analyse how they might support your reflective journey.

You should now be feeling less like you have fallen down a rabbit hole of reflective practice and much like Alice in Wonderland, are beginning to feel curiouser and curiouser about your professional journey working towards a real sense of belonging and thriving as you enter the final chapters of *The Little Book of Reflective Practice.*

4 Belonging and Thriving

Introduction

Welcome to the final chapter of *The Little Book of Reflective Practice*, and it is here I hope you are now beginning to really feel, understand and appreciate not only who you are as an individual but who you are as a reflective practitioner/educator. You may have travelled through the pages of this book and find yourself at the final chapter, but this is certainly not the end of your reflective journey.

It is at this point in your reflective journey that I wish to take you on an imaginary guided tour of my garden of belonging and thriving, a garden where all the flowers, both tall and short, and all the creatures that either fly or crawl (and even the ones that sting), all wish to feel a sense of belonging. Much like the bumble bees that only visit the garden briefly in the Summer, when they do visit, they are much like us humans, in our professional lives, we want to stop a while in a place where we feel we belong and can thrive.

As educators, we need to reflect upon how we ensure we discover who we are, how we create spaces and opportunities to reflect and moreover how we embed reflective theory into our written critical reflections. Furthermore, we

DOI: 10.4324/9781003174851-5

also need to find time to possibly wire or rewire our emotions some days, find energy and magic in environments of ease where we are nurtured to re-energise, develop, dance and sing amongst pots of reflection. So, take a little time now to reflect upon some of the imaginary pots in my garden and pause, reflect and contemplate upon their importance in helping me and you to feel a sense of belonging and thriving.

My Garden of Belonging and Thriving

As you step outside my back door, you will find a small garden, nothing grand, nothing opulent, just a garden! However, what you will find are lots of little pots, pots that have travelled from house to house with me over the years, pots that have weathered or been kicked over and cracked by my now older children. The one thing they all have in common is they all have a story to tell and in my head they all represent my sense of belonging and thriving.

As you step outside the back door into my garden, the very first pot you would find would be the Creative and Expression Pot. Creativity is something that at times in my life as an educator, has been squashed and in doing so crushes my style of teaching and learning, my personality and so it is here as part of my self-reflection, that I recognise I need to belong to a community, a culture, and/or work in an environment that celebrates and recognises my creativity so that I feel a sense of belonging, where I can be me, where I can thrive.

The term 'expressive' acknowledges the fact that as adults, we are almost gardeners in the lives of the young children and adults that we may educate, cultivating learning through creativity and reflection in an environment that celebrates individuality and expression. So, it is in this chapter, that I invite you to spend some time exploring your inner creativity as you produce an Ikigai and begin to consider how you reflect with others and feel a sense of belonging and how you might interact with your reflective buddy to thrive.

A little further along my garden path that leads to the grass, you will find my Little Pot of Community and Connections. If this pot were to have flowers it would possibly be the sort of flowers that you see in hanging baskets (I am no good with flower names), flowers that trail, flowers that go in different directions but always looking to face the sun. It is here, that I believe you will find your community, build connections and work with your reflective buddy as part of your reflective journey, but a little advice from me too you, always look for people who lift your soul, people who turn their faces to the sun looking for rays of sunshine in their working day and professional lives, these will be the people who will observe your reflective journey, praise you and watch you grow and thrive.

There are many other pots in my garden, but I cannot let you travel to the final chapter without introducing you to my favourite pot by the garden shed, The Flawed Pot.

This is the pot that my husband always wants to throw away every spring as we tidy the garden, but it is this pot that I find the most engaging, the pot that reminds me of my own flaws and imperfections. It is the pot that brings me the most magic and reminds me that as an educator, I need to continuously reflect upon my professional practice, to engage with my connections and my community to ensure I feel a sense of belonging which allows me to explore, grow and thrive as much as I wish your reflective journey to be one that brings you joy, belonging and growth.

Theme 4a – Reflecting With Others

A lot of what we have covered so far has been about your self-reflection, reflective theories and how to begin reflective writing but it is also clear that as practitioners we should use feedback from others to increase our self-awareness, we should view our reflections through others' lenses so that we can begin to thrive during our academic, reflective and professional journey. We also need to become risk takers.

If you recall at the beginning of the book, I talked about bungee jumping and how reflection and reflective writing can feel a little scary and maybe much like younger children we need be more childlike and less fearful of the risks we take in our learning and development. We need to be more proactive in taking risks in our professional practice, our reflections and be mindful that it really does not matter how slowly you travel along this reflective journey, it is more important that you do not stop.

However, sometimes we would like a little company on our reflective journey, and this may be a peer, mentor, coach or family member or a critical friend. This is where we can revisit and reimagine the little pot of community and connections and how we might need one connection more so than any other to support us in our understanding of our reflective journey, someone who will offer you a different perspective on your experience: this is who I would call your reflective buddy.

A reflective buddy is supportive, a nurturer and someone who emphasises with your situations, experiences and reflections and whilst they might offer some critique to your reflections it is important that whilst they challenge your thinking, they are non-judgemental and offer you prompts to review, critique and analyse your reflections, all of which will inform your reflective accounts. A reflective buddy is someone who listens without interrupting and appreciates your thinking processes and who gives you time to pause, ponder and contemplate.

I have been a reflective buddy to so many learners and adults in my career that I have begun to develop a deeper understanding and appreciation of what I believe an effective reflective buddy is. In addition to someone who provides you with the time and a reflective space that has moments of silence and effective communication, the reflective buddy also has several qualities that they bring to the reflective space and reflective conversations.

Theme 4b – The Reflective Buddy

We all have a best friend or at least a good friend we can turn to in times of trouble, and this is usually someone who is caring, kind and honest, qualities you would wish for in a reflective buddy, so it is vitally important you choose your reflective buddy carefully and once you do so, you work together to build a solid supportive, working and reflective relationship.

 Reflective Thoughts

Consider who to approach as a reflective buddy.
Have they got the time to support your needs?
What core qualities do you feel a reflective buddy should have?
What part do you play in this working relationship?
Begin to reflect upon your own qualities and how you will be open to suggestions, solutions and other perspectives.

I have taken time to reflect and review my own thoughts as to what qualities a reflective buddy should have and firstly, I decided I would not choose one of my closest friends as I feel they would not be critical or constructive enough for fear of upsetting me and so my reflective conversations may lack the review, analysing and criticality I need to improve my reflections and my reflective accounts.

My Reflective Buddy Would Need to Be

Honest
Respectful
Transparent
Warm and Friendly
Trustworthy
Empathetical
Positive and Constructive

Moreover, I reflected upon the Rainbow Educator introduced to you earlier in the book and decided that there are many of the key components within this educator, that I also consider as key qualities for my reflective buddy. For example, I would wish for my reflective buddy to be versatile, to be able to rearrange our reflective conversations when I possibly cannot make a meeting due to other commitments. I would also wish my reflective buddy to display integrity and be loyal, particularly if I were to open many hidden areas, unknown to me, during our reflective conversations. Take some more time now to consider the qualities you feel a reflective buddy should have. This will also give you the opportunity to reflect upon your own qualities once more and prepare you to possibly be a reflective buddy to a peer or work colleague.

Reflective Thoughts

How do your reflective buddy qualities match mine?

Begin to plan to approach and book a time with your reflective buddy.

Prepare for your meeting, take your journal, ideas and reflections with you.

Once you have read the next theme – Reflective Conversations and the Reflective Buddy, plan and prepare for your reflective conversation.

Theme 4c – Reflective Conversations: Seven Steps to Reflective Success

Once you have a reflective buddy you can begin to connect with one another and plan to meet regularly for your reflective conversations. However, like most conversations there needs to be some structure and/or an awareness of our roles so that the reflective conversation generates solutions, deeper thinking and of course reflective thoughts.

As a result, I created the **Seven Steps to Reflective Success,** a sort of mini guide that I use as a reflective buddy.

The Seven Steps to Reflective Success Are

Share

Your reflective buddy should set aside time and create a reflective space for you to share your immediate reflections and responses to your experiences.

Silence and Space

Your initial reflections and responses to your recent experience should not be rushed. You should feel at ease to recall your reflections at a pace that suits you and, in this moment, it may be that you need space and silence. Silence is powerful, silence gives you time and space to connect learning, to process your emotions and gather your thoughts so your reflective buddy and you should feel comfortable in the power of silence.

For example, I am a highly reflective individual and I have been observed teaching so many times, but I can never respond to the observer instantly after my observation. I need time, space and silence, to process my thoughts, my emotions and my reflections in and on action, and so I have learnt to ask my observer, my reflective buddy, to leave me for a while, give me space, slow down the reflective process and let me share my reflections a little later.

Search and Seek

It is at this point your reflective buddy will listen to your thoughts before you both enter a reflective conversation that is of equal dialogue. Your reflective buddy will listen and then together you will negotiate how to begin your reflective conversation, a conversation where your reflective buddy supports you to search for further analysis, reviewing or critiquing of your recent experiences. In this space, your reflective buddy will also guide you to seek out assumptions you may have made and guide you in reflecting forward.

Shine a Light

This is my favourite part of the reflective conversation, often called the lightbulb moment, but I like to call it the 'shine a light' moment. It is the moment in the reflective conversation where equally you shine a light on one or more parts of the experience, and it is once an area is illuminated that you can then discuss this part of the reflection further and begin to formulate a plan to move forward to the next stage of your reflection.

Solutions

Having shone a light on one or more parts of your experience/s within your reflective conversation you can now begin to search for one or more solutions. This is your reflecting forward, possibly reacting to other lenses, using feedback to then set goals for your future development. Although, at this point I must admit I really do not like setting goals or goal-setting so let us call it solution busting! And that is it – you should now be ready to reflect forward, to solution bust and to begin the reflective conversation and ripple all over again.

Final Thoughts

You are now at the point in your reflective journey where you can begin to plan when your reflective conversations can and will take place and how you will potentially use all or some of the Seven Steps to Reflective Success that you have been introduced to. Both this chapter to date and Chapter 2 – Reflective Writing will support you in your planning, drafting and writing of your critically reflective accounts as you now begin the final part of your journey – Thriving.

Theme 4d – Finding Your Ikigai

Once you have had several reflective conversations with your reflective buddy you should be feeling empowered and enlightened to begin to reflect forward and begin to consider your future growth and development. It is here I wish to remind you that you should now invest some time in exploring a few strategies that may help you begin to identify your needs, areas of development and what opportunities you still need to explore as we set out to ponder, pause, reflect and contemplate and travel from the BEING ME, to the belonging and thriving.

Let me start by taking you back inside my brain. It is fair to say that most days it is jumbled with a thousand thoughts, a few to do lists and as mentioned earlier in the book, often resembles the roots of a tree which are entangled and a little chaotic trying find a way to lay a foundation for growth. But it is when I pause, reflect and contemplate that I give my brain the opportunity to untangle and reflect, to sort through the day's events, the observations I may have made, the activities I may have undertaken and my writing. It is in these moments of chaos that I return to my Ikigai.

What Is an Ikigai?

Ikigai is a Japanese concept that means your reason for being and is best defined as 'your purpose in life and loosely translated is Japanese for to live (iki) and the reason (gai).

For those of you who know me, or have been taught by me, know that I have a real passion for psychology and philosophy, and it is here where my thinking and my continuous return to my Ikigai is of importance to my being and at times when my brain becomes tangled, my purpose mis-aligned or the actions of others cause me contemplation, I stop, pause, reflect and contemplate my Ikigai. More simply maybe just take a moment now to stop, pause and reflect upon the following question.

What is that one thing you get up for in the morning, aside from your family, your professional purpose and meaning? This is the start of your Ikigai.

An Ikigai is a kind of Venn diagram and where the sections converge, this is your IKIGAI.

 Reflective Thoughts

Ask yourself:

1. What do you love? What is your passion?
2. What does the world need? What is your mission?
3. What are you good at?
4. What can you get paid for?

One thing I will add is that I do believe that you should revisit your Ikigai regularly, you may find as you develop in your academic and professional journey, your purpose may change, you may develop new skills you are good at, and you may even rethink your mission and your purpose in life.

As a pastoral lead and coach in most of my education roles, I have used this concept with both learners in tutorials and with staff in appraisals and development.

Now it is your turn to invest in yourself and start your THRIVING journey, so go ahead start creating YOUR IKIGAI.

Reflective Activity

How to create an Ikigai

You can either draw your own Venn diagram or use the template provided. You begin by taking time to think of answers to the following questions for each section of the Venn diagram.

Take a few minutes to read the questions in each section and then begin to write any key words, ideas or phrases and quotes that you feel belong in each large outer circle.

Now look to see if any of the areas overlap. Some of the answers to the questions you have written may begin to intersect.

It is then you need to pause, ponder and reflect upon how any of the intersections are balanced in your personal ikigai, are there similarities. For example, I love creativity and I can use this and have used this as part of my career. My love of creativity has brought me money and joy. It is here you could go on to be honest with yourself, for example let us imagine I found myself in a role or culture where I could not utilise my creativity, I would have to rethink my mission and my purpose, revisit my Ikigai.

Completing the Ikigai will hopefully give you a vision and provide you with the key to your thriving with a purpose towards your chosen career.

Finally, remember that your purpose in life is not fixed and so revisit your Ikigai regularly.

Questions to reflect upon and answer:

What you love?

What do you find fun, interesting and in turn really motivates you?

What is it that sparks energy and enthusiasm for you?

What could you enthusiastically talk about for hours on end or what activities could you do that you would never bore of?

What is it that the world needs?

This question is meant to guide you in figuring out what you can give to the world. This seems quite a big ask so maybe if this is overwhelming, break it down and think about what you have to give to the sector you wish to work in. For example, I would answer maybe nurturing, empathy and creativity. You can possibly see here already that in my Ikigai, the love of creativity and what I believe the sector needs is already an intersection and something for me to reflect upon in my Ikigai.

What issues do you feel that your chosen sector has, or your community that you might like to solve?

What Are You Good At?

This question is about being BRAVE and honest and asks you to embrace and maybe shout out a bit loud about your skills and talents which you may be hiding. For example, not many people know I am a qualified florist and I retrained in the evenings outside of work hours so that I could follow my natural creativity. I went on to use this skill delivering some evening classes, where I did not get paid (I could have done and identified in my Ikigai), but this was something I did because I identified that I love art, and I was good at floristry and as it was my passion, I felt it was something I could give to my local community.

So, consider the following questions:

What parts of your current job/role or training do you find effortless?
What do you find brings you joy and is a skill?
What talents do you have?
Also, consider if you were to maybe have some more training or experiences, what could you be your very best at?

What Can You Be Paid For?

This question may make you feel uncomfortable, but we all need to pay our bills and so let us consider what it is that you can be paid for?

What have you been paid for lately?
What could you be paid for? Do you need any extra skills or training for this career/job?

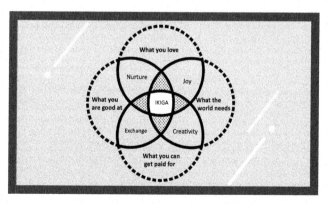

Final Thoughts

Having completed this exercise, you may not have found your Ikigai immediately and that is perfectly okay. It may be that you need to return to this and take more time to think about the process as a whole and the questions within each section.

A couple of things you should take away with you is to always try to be more lion as discussed earlier and try new things. You might find sections and intersections of your Ikigai move. For example, I never set out with the plan to teach adults. I was always convinced I would only ever teach Early Years, but it was by using courage and displaying many components of the Rainbow Educator that I have changed many sections and intersections of my Ikigai and have found myself on many new and exciting paths.

Finding your Ikigai, finding yourself is a constant process towards our journey to thriving.

Theme 4e – SWOT Analysis

It may be that creating an Ikigai was not the process for you and so an alternative to this is to create a SWOT analysis.

SWOT is an acronym for your Strengths, Weaknesses, Opportunities and Threats and can be completed at any point in your professional and academic journey. It may be that you produce just one or you revisit this activity periodically. It may also prove useful for you to take one along to a reflective buddy session and/or to share one with your tutor, coach or mentor.

A SWOT analysis is a strategic and useful framework to guide you in identifying and building upon your strengths, addressing areas that you need to develop. I tend not to use the word weaknesses, I prefer to call them areas of development.

A SWOT analysis will also help you to identify and begin to set out a plan as to how to take advantage of any possible opportunities within your course and/or training, that will support your growth and development, before finally helping you to recognise possible risks and how you might minimise these. Risks always sound a bit terrifying, but a risk might be something like time. For example, I know that I cannot take on any more projects at the time of writing this book as it would be a threat to writing and completing this book which you are now reading! (Thank You)

However, you choose to use a SWOT analysis is up to you. You might want to complete one and keep it to yourself and keep it in your reflective journal, you may wish to do one and share the information with your reflective buddy or you might wish to complete one to share with your tutor/mentor, where together you could then use the analysis to create and set some future goals (or solution busters) for your learning and professional development.

Reflective Activity

Strengths	Weaknesses
Opportunities	Threats

Strengths

Start with your strengths and do not be modest. We are very good at under selling ourselves. This is the part of the SWOT analysis where you need to list all your relevant strengths.

Take time to think and list your skills, your experiences, any elements of your personality and relevant career qualifications or abilities you feel are relevant.

Weaknesses

Use this section to reflect upon any areas you feel may be a weakness in your application of learning, your vocational practice and/or training. Please see this as an opportunity to create a list which you can analyse and develop.

Opportunities

In this section, spend some time thinking of the bigger picture here and consider external factors. Consider all the opportunities you may have for further training to enhance your learning and development. In this section, you can also list resources you may have access to that will provide further opportunities for you.

Threats

Finally, you need to identify any threats that may present themselves in your present or future journey. These will be things that may hinder your learning and development.

Once you have completed all four sections, you can now review your SWOT analysis. Look and see if your strengths and opportunities outweigh the weaknesses, or if you have some potential threats which could and can be supported and how you will seek this support. Your completed SWOT analysis is then ready for you to maybe share with your tutor, coach and/or mentor in supporting your future development.

Theme 4f – Feedback and Developmental Needs

As we almost reach the end of *The Little Book of Reflective Practice* and having completed an Ikigai and/or a SWOT, you may now be reflecting upon your future needs and be contemplating how you will continue to thrive, so this is where you will spend some time exploring the importance of and the role of feedback. Moreover, feedback plus your own self-reflection will have also given you the opportunity to begin to plan your future developmental needs.

At this stage, it is worthwhile reminding yourself of the previous contents of the book, such as the Johari Window approach from Chapter 3, as well as creating an Ikigai, completing a SWOT analysis and the role of the reflective buddy and reflective conversations (Chapter 4), all of which will have provided you with the chance to not only increase your self-awareness but also to begin to consider how to use feedback from others within your community of practice.

By now you will have possibly received feedback from your reflective buddy, your mentor, tutor or coach as well as some possible reflections and feedback using Brookfield's lenses (Chapter 3).

Feedback

Using all the feedback from dialogues, reflective conversations and your reflective accounts and feedback will help you to begin to understand how feedback should be used not only for ongoing development but how it can help you in other ways.

Reflective Activity

This activity requires you to think and evidence feedback.

Under each section you can evidence and write where you have received feedback relating to each area and how this feedback has supported you.

Motivation – What feedback have you received that has been motivational?

How has this feedback inspired you? How can you evidence this?

Performance – What feedback have you received that you feel has helped you to reflect on action, to reflect forward and has improved your performance or your academic skills?

How has this feedback then related to your professional development? Can you evidence this?

Constructive Criticism – Areas of Improvement

How has feedback supported you to improve in a particular area? Be specific and give an example.

Be honest – How did you feel receiving this constructive criticism?

List any developmental needs that you still need to develop and have been identified because of feedback.

Challenge– Can you explain the importance of feedback in all these areas? How? Why?

How does engaging in a reflective conversation or equal dialogue with your reflective buddy support your professional development?

Developmental Needs

As you have come this far into the book, you may have come to appreciate that a lot of my work is influenced by lessons from Japanese psychology and so let me introduce you to one more new word, 'kaizen', whose generic interpretation, and definition is 'improvement'. And so as you enter the final stage of thriving it is imperative that you take steps to improve yourself and identify your developmental needs and there are several ways in which you can enhance your professional learning and development.

There are several educational acronyms for improvement and development, such as CPD, Continuous Professional Development or PDP, a Professional Development Plan, whichever acronym is used by your educational establishment, training provider or workplace they all require you to take steps to 'improve', 'kaizen'.

The first step towards your improvement is to identify your developmental needs and by this point you should have been able to identify these either through feedback and/or through undertaking exercises such as the SWOT analysis. Once you have identified your developmental needs, the next step is to appreciate the importance of acting, this may be discussing your needs with your reflective buddy, your tutor, your mentor and/or coach or your employee. It is worth noting that CPD or any kind of improvement does not have to be a course or a formal qualification. For example, you can demonstrate improvement and document your engagement with a wide range of activities that you may not have considered as CPD.

*Continuous Professional Development Can Include All
or Some of the Following*

Social Media – For example, I have made lots of professional connections through Twitter which has led to my involvement in research projects, reading groups or attendance of a wide range of free courses.

External Courses, Additional Qualifications, Workshops and/or External Training – There is a wide range of courses available and a mixture of paid and free.

Choose wisely and do your homework. For example, is the trainer well qualified and insured to deliver the courses? It is also worth noting that you do not want to enrol in another qualification or a course that runs over several weeks if your time management framework clearly shows you are limited for time.

Conferences

Shadowing and/or Observing Peers – This is an invaluable experience, and it is free!

Ask your peers if you can observe their practice and you will find there is always something that you will take away with you to reflect upon. Equally, you should be open your peers observing/shadowing you and you should view this as a positive experience as the feedback will be useful to feed into your reflective account. Remember those peers' lenses (Brookfield) and your hidden area (Johari Window). Both theories/approaches will feed seamlessly into your reflective accounts simply by some shadowing or observing and in turn you are 'improving'.

Visits to Settings – This will need clearance from your tutor/mentor, but you may be fortunate to have a vocational setting or an organised placement/training for your course and absolutely everything you do within this setting/training is part of your CPD. Just do not forget to log it!

Reading and Research - Reading is something that is outstanding for your professional development and improvement. Try to read beyond a reading list that may have been set for you. Often I have read a mixture of fiction and non-fiction and elements of both have informed by practice and led me to write, publish or create a resource.

Research is something you do day in, day out in your professional practice, possibly without realising it, but go one step further, and let's say something fascinates you, a topic, or a theme, then go and research it further or look out for others who are currently researching this area of interest, read and research their work. You could also become involved in a small piece of action research as part of your professional learning and development.

One key for improvement is Quality not Quantity.

Choose Quality over Quantity and do not forget to log it. *(Use the CPD template in this book to log your improvement.)*

Now you have a list of ideas for your development needs, it is worth spending some time looking back at your feedback to date and reflecting upon what improvement you need and how you will do this and as you do, be mindful that there several reasons why you are asked to undertake CPD.

CPD can be personalised, generic and/or mandatory.

CPD can be an event that you attend alone or as a whole team. For example, if there are any recent regulatory requirements or changes in legislation, then the whole team will need to attend so that you are kept up to date with how these changes may affect your policies and procedures.

In addition to this, you should be considering how you will meet your developmental needs so that you are maintaining your own knowledge and skills. For example, I was a NNEB, and I no longer work in Early Years, however, to ensure that my knowledge and skills are up to date, I not only attend training, conferences, read and undertake research, but also volunteer in a local Nursery. My volunteering involves training the staff when I can, but also means I am part of an Early Years team. I can observe practice, I can make contributions to children's learning and development, I can make meaningful contributions to the team and the wider society, and I can most definitely still wipe the odd nose! Moreover, this CPD supports my CV, improves my progression, and informs my teaching but most importantly for me it lets me be ME! A Reflective Nursery Nurse.

This is an extract from Lisa Broome, the manager of a Nursery I support with their CPD. Her extract covers the perspective of her role as a manager and her personal reflection of working with her team and how CPD meets the developmental needs of her team.

 Reflective Thoughts

Read the reflection and pause and reflect how you may wish to revisit the Rainbow Educator. Revisit feedback you received and then begin to complete your CPD, work and/or vocational experiences, your reflections and the possible impact each experience has had upon your professional learning and development.

As an Early Years Manager of many years, there's one acronym that fills me with dread, CPD. It is essential and integral to our profession and ongoing expertise, but it had become such a repetitive experience. The body language from the team when it is mentioned ranged from tight lips, teeth clenching, chair shuffling, finger tapping and the blatantly obvious eye rolling. I would pioneer onwards promoting many training sessions as 'best practice', 'personal development' and a deluge of positive outcomes that I am assuming will be gained as a result. Staff placated me with their gathered enthusiasm and agreed to engage with the latest training schedule or session, they attend dutifully and it 'ticks the CPD box'. Albeit they did return with a new local authority initiative or focus, they rarely felt that it has impacted on their personal practice or expertise.

I had to agree, I was torn between being a conscientious leader promoting CPD and listening to my team, a team who are experienced and passionate in all that they do. I have always listened to my team, before anything else, and it resonated with me that I needed to source something unique to inspire all.

This was the point when something magical happened, I had re-connected with Annie Pendrey, a personal connection from my own educational journey. Annie had been my first Foundation Degree Lecturer. After many messages and discussions (we had a lot of catching up to do) it was agreed that Annie would connect with my team, and we would focus on some bespoke CPD. The magic began, continued to work together to design bespoke reflective practice that was bursting with energy and creativity.

Annie 'sparkled' her way through zoom sessions, inspiring us with her unique Rainbow Practitioner reflective focus, at last we had finally found our inspiration. The work resonated with us all at every level, it was original, authentic, and it reflected our passion in Early Years.

The team were encouraged to self-reflect, no hidden agenda, no new Government initiative, just to simply connect with themselves as practitioners. These simple connections created an energy within the setting, the realisation that each one of them had special qualities that they could recognise comfortably and with confidence. This renewed energy was tangible, I could feel it within the everyday practice, parental engagement and multi-agency working. The team were 'walking taller' and this was a joy to see throughout such a difficult time, they needed a 'rainbow boost', as did I.

We continue to work reflectively with Annie, the Rainbow Educator has become embedded in all that we do. As we move forwards towards the revised EYFS changes we will use our CPD 'tool kit' to embrace challenges with creativity and reflection.

Continued Professional Development is no longer an area of dread or a repetitive drain, it has now become inspirational and creative, the body language is now positive, smiles and hand clapping! As a leader this is a joy to behold, to see and feel that my team value and recognise their individual expertise and qualities is priceless.

Logging Your CPD and Reflections

Use and/or create a table to make notes and log your CPD, work and/or vocational experiences.

You may wish to add, delete or amend the headings but take time to capture all the experiences and CPD you undertake. We sometimes forget all the wonderful interactions and experiences we undertake and for me I think the most important part of this log is noting the impact that any of the experiences have had upon your professional learning and development.

This information is vital for your reflections and to add to your CV and as evidence in interviews.

CPD, Work and/or Vocational Experiences					
Date	Organisation	Name of the Course	Overview of the Content	The Impact of the Training.	Your Reflection

Just One More Thing

Well done, you did it, you have travelled through the pages of *The Little Book of Reflective Practice* and hopefully you are much more informed about the art of reflection and how to begin discovering who you are as an individual and as a professional.

Equally, I hope you have begun to feel you belong and are part of a reflective community where you can thrive and continue your reflective practice, but there is just one more thing I wish to say and that is . . .

'A journey of a thousand miles begins with the first step' Lao Tzu

Keep Reflecting!

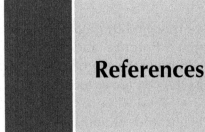

References

Boud, D., Keogh, R., & Walker, D. (1985) *Reflection: Turning Experience into Learning*. Oxon, UK: Routledge.

Brookfield, S. (1994) *Becoming a Critically Reflective Teacher*. San-Francisco, CA: Jossey-Bass.

Gibbs, G. (1998) *Learning by Doing: A Guide to Teaching and Learning through Reflective Practice*. London: Routledge David Fulton Press.

Kolb, D. (1984) *Experiential Learning as the Science of Learning and Development*. New Jersey: Prentice Hall.

Luft, J., & Ingham, H. (1955) *The Johari Window: A Graphic Model of Interpersonal Awareness*. University of California, Los Angeles, Extension Office, Proceedings of the Western Training Laboratory in Group Development.

Schön, D. A. (1983) *The Reflective Practitioner*. San Francisco, CA: Jossey-Bass.

Adjectives to Support the Reflective Activities

Rainbow Educator – Theme 1d
Johari Window – Theme 3f

Adjectives
There may be some adjectives you need to define first.

Accepting	Adaptable	Bold
Calm	Cheerful	Complex
Clever	Charismatic	Confident
Creative	Dependable	Dignified
Energetic	Experienced	Flexible
Extroverted	Friendly	Fair
Giving	Generous	Happy
Helpful	Honest	Idealistic
Independent	Ingenious	Intelligent
Introverted	Innovative	Kind
Knowledgeable	Logical	Loving
Loyal	Modest	Nervous
Observant	Organised	Objective
Patient	Professional	Proud
Passionate	Punctual	Quiet
Relaxed	Reflective	Responsive
Shy	Self-conscious	Self-assertive
Spontaneous	Transparent	Tense
Trustworthy	Witty	Wise

You do not only have to use this list; please personalise your choice and add your own adjectives.